"no end to remember

—Henry Ford, as noted in one of his small "jot books"

The Henry Ford

OFFICIAL GUIDEBOOK

DONNA R. BRADEN
Senior Curator & Curator of Public Life

BECKON BOOKS

Contents

the Henry Ford

Benson Ford
Research Center

Giant Screen &
Anderson Theaters

Henry Ford Academy

Welcome to The Henry Ford

When Henry Ford created the Edison Institute, as The Henry Ford was called in 1929, he believed in the importance of learning from the past to create a better future. He believed that people, especially kids and students, should learn history in a hands-on environment—not through textbooks. Most importantly, he believed in the power of objects—artifacts—as sources of inspiration for people to absorb and to use in an effort to make their own mark in this world.

We continue Henry Ford's vision for this institution today.

Our mission is to provide unique educational experiences based on authentic objects, stories, and lives from America's traditions of ingenuity, resourcefulness, and innovation. Our purpose is to inspire people to learn from these traditions to help shape a better future.

At The Henry Ford, we believe we have a responsibility to engage our visitors and treat every person walking through our gates as if they are the next Henry Ford …or Thomas Edison…or Rosa Parks. We believe every individual has the potential to change the world. At The Henry Ford and through our unparalleled collection—the Archive of American Innovation—visitors can discover that potential and be inspired by the authentic objects and stories of the innovators who came before us.

Each person possesses a unique spark, and at The Henry Ford we can provide the ever necessary and important context for innovation that helps people envision a path forward. We often say: Ordinary people have changed the world. You can too.

I hope you find this guide to be a useful and informative product that gives a deeper understanding of this institution's founding and founder. I thank you so much for visiting The Henry Ford. Please visit us often, and we look forward to your return.

Patricia E. Mooradian

Patricia E. Mooradian
President
The Henry Ford

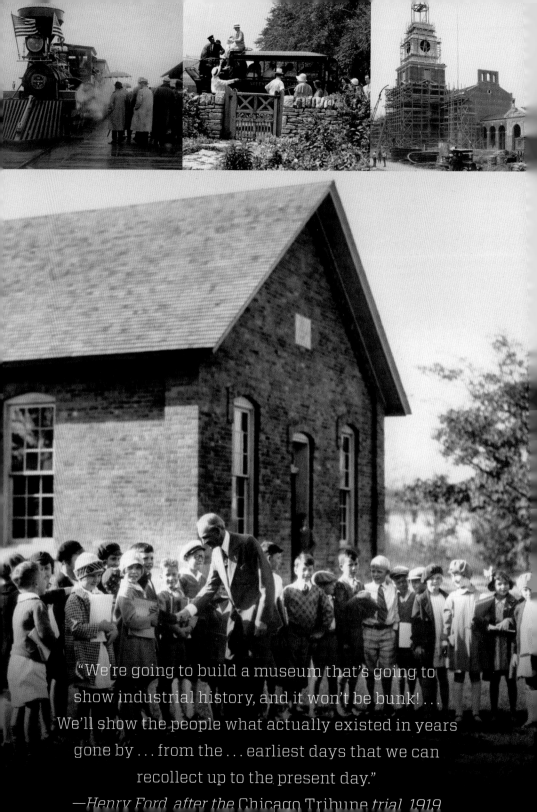

"We're going to build a museum that's going to
show industrial history, and it won't be bunk!...
We'll show the people what actually existed in years
gone by ... from the ... earliest days that we can
recollect up to the present day."

—Henry Ford, after the Chicago Tribune trial, 1919

Introduction

lthough Henry Ford became one of the world's wealthiest and most powerful industrialists, he never forgot the values of the rural life he had left behind growing up on a farm. As early as 1905, he was accumulating items associated with his hero Thomas Edison and his own personal history. But the collecting bug really started in 1914, as he began searching for McGuffey *Eclectic Readers* to verify a long-remembered verse from one of his old grade school lessons.

In 1916, a series of three articles in the *Chicago Tribune* attacked Henry Ford for his support of United States pacifism during World War I. These articles called Ford an "anarchist" and an "ignorant idealist." One article quoted him as saying, "History is more or less 'bunk'" (implying that it was boring or nonsense). Ford sued the *Tribune* for libel. At the trial that ensued, lawyers trying to prove Ford's "ignorance" mercilessly examined him on a variety of schoolbook topics, especially history. As Ford answered question after question incorrectly, he replied in exasperation, "I did not say it was bunk. It was bunk to me."

Henry Ford never really believed that history was bunk. What he believed *was* bunk was the kind of history taught in schools—that emphasized kings and generals and omitted the lives of ordinary folks. The trial inspired Ford to build a museum that would show people this kind of history. Before long, he was accumulating not only items connected with his heroes and his own past, but

1919 newspaper article covering Henry Ford's libel suit

Opposite: Henry Ford greets students on the opening day of his new experimental school, September 16, 1929.

also objects showing what he called the "development of American industry" and items related to ordinary people and everyday life.

In 1919, Henry Ford learned that his birthplace was at risk because of a road improvement project. He took charge, moving the farmhouse and restoring it to the way he remembered it from the time of his mother's death in 1876, when he was thirteen. He and his assistants combed the countryside for items that he remembered. He followed up by restoring the one-room school he had attended as a boy, Scotch Settlement School; the 1686 Wayside Inn in South Sudbury, Massachusetts (as part of a plan to develop a "working" colonial village there); and the 1836 Botsford Inn, a stagecoach inn where he and his wife, Clara, had once attended old-fashioned dances. These restorations gave Ford many opportunities to add to his rapidly growing collections while honing ideas for his own historic village.

During the 1920s, Ford's collection grew in leaps and bounds. Once people learned he was collecting objects for a museum, they flooded his office with letters offering to give or sell him items they felt had historical value. He also sent out assistants to help him acquire the kinds of objects he felt were important to preserve.

For his museum in Dearborn, Michigan, Ford envisioned two separate facilities. An indoor museum would tell the story of man's technological progress through comprehensive displays, while an outdoor village would show how these types of objects were made and used. In 1926, Ford scouted out sites for his museum and village, ultimately choosing a parcel of land in Dearborn—right in the middle of where he lived and worked.

Thomas Edison, Henry Ford, and Edison's former lab assistant Francis Jehl in Menlo Park Laboratory during Light's Golden Jubilee, October 21, 1929

Ford decided on October 21, 1929, as the dedication date for the Museum and Village—a date that marked the fiftieth anniversary of Thomas Edison's invention of his workable incandescent lamp. On the night of this so-called Light's Golden Jubilee celebration, crowds cheered as President Hoover, Edison, and Ford ceremoniously arrived in a train pulled by an 1850s locomotive. After an elegant dinner in the Museum, the three men went out to the restored Menlo Park

Village entrance building, 1934

Laboratory in Greenfield Village. There, the eighty-two-year-old Edison re-created the lighting of his incandescent lamp. The event was broadcast live over national radio. Henry Ford named his new complex The Edison Institute of Technology to honor his friend and longtime hero.

Early on, Henry Ford's vision for the Museum and Village was to provide hands-on learning opportunities for students. Ford's philosophy of education was "learn to do by doing." This was the way he had learned during his own childhood—the way that he himself learned best. In the experimental Edison Institute schools he founded in Greenfield Village in 1929, students learned not only from books, but also from objects and hands-on experiences.

As the number of people requesting tours through the expanding Village grew from about four hundred a day in 1929 to nearly one thousand by 1933 (some were admitted, many were turned away), Ford agreed to officially open the doors. A visitors' gatehouse was completed in May, and on June 22, 1933, the public was admitted. Although it was not finished, the Museum welcomed its first official visitors about a week later. By the late 1930s, over five hundred thousand people had visited the Village and Museum, including royalty, Hollywood stars, and American industrialists.

Henry Ford continued to collect objects for the Museum and to add homes, mills, and shops to the Village. By the time of his death in 1947, Henry Ford had collected a slice of the American past unmatched in size and scope. Since that time, staff members of The Henry Ford have continued to build upon Ford's one-of-a-kind collection, enlarging and broadening its scope into what today we call the Archive of American Innovation.

1927 Ford Tri-Motor airplane

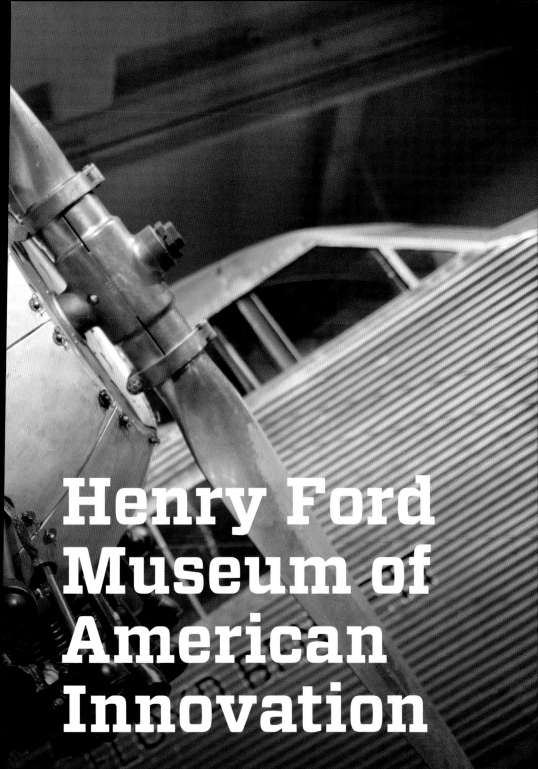

Henry Ford
Museum of
American
Innovation

"I'm going to start up a museum and give people a
true picture of the development of the country."

Henry Ford Museum of American Innovation

Henry Ford envisioned a large indoor museum to house and display his growing collection. When Detroit-trained architect Robert O. Derrick proposed a façade featuring a replica of Philadelphia's Independence Hall, Ford immediately took to the idea. In Ford's mind, this historic building—a recognizable symbol of American freedom and democracy—was linked to the ideals that made possible many of the objects he planned to display inside.

In 1928, he commissioned Derrick to pursue the Independence Hall design in front with a huge open exhibition hall in back. On September 27 of that year, Ford watched as his hero Thomas Edison thrust agriculturist Luther Burbank's spade into a wet concrete block, then inscribed his own signature into the concrete. To Ford, this act symbolized the union of agriculture and industry—cornerstones of America's economy and a key principle Ford wished to illustrate in his museum.

The concept of innovation lies at the heart of the multitude of objects on display in the Henry Ford Museum of American Innovation. While *inventions* imply initial solutions to problems or improvements upon earlier ideas, *innovations* are game changers. They involve solving a problem in a brand new way with such far-reaching impact that they render old ways obsolete. As a result, they often radically alter how people think about themselves, their social interactions, and the larger world.

Opposite: In 1967, this Ford Mark IV race car won the world's most important sports car race—the 24 Hours of Le Mans.

This 1823 engraved copy of the Declaration of Independence was created when it became apparent that the precious original was noticeably fading.

Social Transformation

S ocial transformation involves a shift in the collective consciousness of a society. It occurs when people create change through new patterns of behavior or social action. This can include political shifts, social movements, economic change, changing systems of beliefs and values, new patterns of racial relations, or a rethinking of personal and collective identities.

The ideal of freedom—as laid out in the Declaration of Independence, protected by the Constitution, and continually reinterpreted over time—lies at the heart of the American nation. This ideal has been embodied by the passionate voices and courageous action of people willing to stand up for their beliefs.

The Museum's *With Liberty and Justice for All* exhibition explores the concept of social transformation as it evolved through four key transformative eras during which American freedom was tested, contested, and ultimately redefined: the Revolutionary War era, the Civil War era, the woman's suffrage movement, and the civil rights movement. The objects highlighted here epitomize Americans' ongoing struggle for freedom.

A national procession for woman's suffrage, Washington, DC, 1913. Women gained the right to vote in 1919.

Engraved Copy of the Declaration of Independence

AMERICAN COLONISTS CRIED "no taxation without representation" to Great Britain's continual attempts to tax them in order to raise funds after 1763. When representatives from the American colonies met together in July 1776, a majority felt that the time was right to declare independence from Great Britain. Thomas Jefferson had drafted a Declaration of Independence—borrowing from ancient sources, other political thinkers, members of the Continental Congress, and treatises he had already written. This document became a bold vision for freedom and human rights that inspired leaders like Abraham Lincoln and continues to inspire people today.

By 1820, Secretary of State John Quincy Adams had become concerned over the fragile condition of the original Declaration of Independence document after so many years of handling. With the approval of Congress, he commissioned engraver William J. Stone to produce a facsimile of this precious document using a copper plate. In 1823, Congress ordered two hundred copies of this engraved version to be printed on parchment. This is one of those copies.

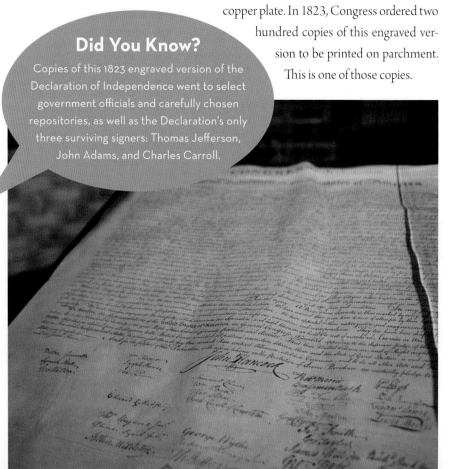

Did You Know?

Copies of this 1823 engraved version of the Declaration of Independence went to select government officials and carefully chosen repositories, as well as the Declaration's only three surviving signers: Thomas Jefferson, John Adams, and Charles Carroll.

George Washington's Camp Bed

ON JULY 4, 1776, the Continental Congress approved the Declaration of Independence. Now, only large-scale war could decide America's fate. George Washington had already been chosen to lead the Continental army, a ragtag group of patriots with few weapons and no military training. As commander-in-chief of the army, Washington lost more battles than he won. But he was composed, fearless, untiring, and able to learn from his mistakes. As the war wound down, he used this portable foldout bed specially made for him on his tour of battlefields in New York and New England.

By the end of the Revolutionary War, no man was more admired in the United States than George Washington. He could easily have become dictator or king. But he believed in the democratic ideals of the new nation, and he realized that the American government could only work if its power came from the consent of the people. George Washington would remain an enduring symbol of American freedom and democracy.

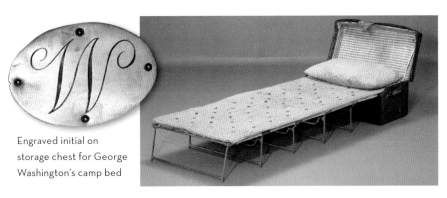

Engraved initial on storage chest for George Washington's camp bed

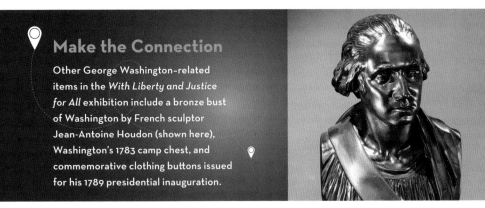

Make the Connection

Other George Washington–related items in the *With Liberty and Justice for All* exhibition include a bronze bust of Washington by French sculptor Jean-Antoine Houdon (shown here), Washington's 1783 camp chest, and commemorative clothing buttons issued for his 1789 presidential inauguration.

The Lincoln Chair

THE NATION WAS BEING TORN APART BY A CIVIL WAR, but President Lincoln was committed to preserving the Union. He believed that the United States was the testing ground for a unique form of democracy. In 1863, his Emancipation Proclamation shifted the goal of the war from being a fight to preserve the Union to one that included freeing the enslaved. With General Robert E. Lee's surrender at Appomattox, Lincoln's vision of a more perfect Union seemed imminent.

However, on the night of April 14, 1865 (only five days after Lee's surrender), President Lincoln was shot while enjoying the play *Our American Cousin* at Ford's Theatre and died the following day. He was sitting in this rocker, which he found comfortable. The nation was stunned. For days afterward, people filed past Lincoln's body as it lay in state in Washington, DC. Then, the body was borne by train to his home in Springfield, Illinois, making stops along the way for grief-stricken Americans to pay their respects.

LOOK CLOSER

Analysis of fabric samples from the chair seems to indicate blood on the right back of the chair and the center front of the seat cushion. Other stains indicate hair oil (top back) and water and plaster damage (bottom back).

Joint Resolution Proposing the Thirteenth Amendment

ON JANUARY 1, 1863, President Abraham Lincoln issued the Emancipation Proclamation in an attempt to counteract severe Union losses during the Civil War. This presidential order granted freedom to all slaves in the Confederacy and helped enlist needed support for the war from antislavery advocates. But it was not a legal document, and Lincoln knew it.

While campaigning for his second presidential term in 1864, Lincoln drafted a document that would legally abolish slavery forever. This became the Thirteenth Amendment to the Constitution, passed by Congress on January 31, 1865. It would take ten more months for the necessary states to ratify this amendment so

it could become law. Unfortunately, President Lincoln did not live to see that happen, nor was this legal document sufficient to ensure African Americans' basic rights.

This is one of a limited number of manuscript copies known to survive of the Joint Resolution proposing the Thirteenth Amendment. It was submitted by Congress and approved by President Lincoln on February 1, 1865.

Past *Forward*

Over the next five years, the Fourteenth and Fifteenth Amendments to the Constitution followed—legally guaranteeing African Americans the basic rights of citizenship and the ability to vote. But these were just legal documents. Enforcing them was another matter, one fraught with violence and discrimination into the next century.

Drinking fountain, 1954

Woman's Suffrage Banner

"REMEMBER THE LADIES," wrote Abigail Adams to her husband, John, in 1776. The Declaration of Independence only stated that all *men* are created equal. But by the mid-1800s, courageous spokeswomen like Elizabeth Cady Stanton and Lucretia Mott were declaring that women deserved the same rights as men.

Two new female leaders emerged during the early 1900s, focusing specifically on the fight for woman's suffrage (the right to vote). Carrie Chapman Catt was a political lobbyist, while Alice Paul was a social agitator. Through their separate efforts, women everywhere—and men too—joined the struggle to gain women suffrage.

Using very different tactics, Catt and Paul offered women from all walks of life a chance to get involved. Women organized parades, printed flyers, and got people to sign petitions. The hard work and unswerving determination of these two leaders and their followers finally led, in 1919, to the passage of the Nineteenth Amendment, granting women the right to vote.

Suffrage banner carried in rallies and marches, 1910

Past *Forward*

Women won the right to vote but still lacked equal rights with men. In 1923, woman's suffrage leader Alice Paul and political activist Crystal Eastman drafted an Equal Rights Amendment. It has been revised and updated many times, but no official amendment has yet been approved. Several organizations continue to address issues of gender inequality.

Equal Rights Amendment button, circa 1972

Rosa Parks Bus

ON THIS MONTGOMERY, ALABAMA, bus on December 1, 1955, soft-spoken African American seamstress Rosa Parks refused to give up her seat to a white man as dictated by existing segregation laws. She was neither the first African American nor the first woman to challenge the segregation laws within the public transportation system. But her flawless character, quiet strength, and moral fortitude ignited action in others. She was also prepared after years of reviewing discrimination cases as the local NAACP secretary and having recently attended a desegregation workshop.

When she was arrested, the African American community knew that this time city officials had "messed with the wrong one." Rosa Parks's act of uncommon courage led to an immediate citywide bus boycott by the African American community. The arrest of Rosa Parks and the bus boycott resulted in the meteoric rise of Dr. Martin Luther King Jr. as the widely recognized leader of the civil rights movement. Over time, Rosa Parks became known internationally as a symbol for human rights.

LOOK CLOSER

Inside the bus, visitors can hear Rosa Parks recount her experiences, excerpted from a later interview. A light shines on the seat she sat in, located behind the front ten seats that were reserved for white riders.

This steam engine, made about 1855,
incorporates both advanced technology and
Gothic decorative details.

Energy and Power

It takes only one power outage for people to realize how fundamental energy is to their daily lives. From the earliest steam engines to modern electrical transmission, power systems have involved a combination of numerous iterative improvements and a few groundbreaking innovations.

Following pioneering developments in Great Britain, Americans' unique advancements in power-generating technologies expanded the country's industrial capacity through the application of energy resources. Although humans, animals, and wind provided power in restricted locations, the plentiful supply of fast-running water powered most early American shops and mills. Over time, steam engines competed with waterwheels to power shops and factories. By the late 1800s, steam had become the dominant prime mover in American industry.

During the early 1900s, increasing demand for energy led to developments in electricity. These evolved from special-purpose systems into large utility stations that supplied power to a uniform national network.

The Museum's *Made in America: Power* exhibition highlights significant innovations in the creation and transmission of power through the use of different energy sources.

The massive Corliss engine shown in this engraving, which powered all the machinery in Machinery Hall at Philadelphia's 1876 Centennial Exhibition, was the crowning achievement of George Corliss's career.

Left: Newcomen engine, made about 1750; right: 1796 Boulton & Watt engine

Newcomen and Watt Steam Engines

THE MUSEUM'S UNPARALLELED COLLECTION of steam engines begins with the Newcomen engine, made around 1750, and the Boulton & Watt engine, built in 1796. Both these British engines were created to pump water.

Named for its inventor Thomas Newcomen, the Newcomen engine is considered to be the oldest surviving steam engine in the world. Thomas Newcomen, a skilled iron mechanic, invented the world's first practical steam engine in 1712. His design combined existing elements and theory with new discoveries. Newcomen engines became phenomenally successful. Hundreds were constructed, built in sizes large enough to pump great quantities of water. Newcomen's engine remained basically unchanged for the next sixty years.

James Watt's improvements to Newcomen's engine, along with further mechanical refinements, increased steam engine efficiency and versatility. In 1777, Watt entered into a partnership with entrepreneur Matthew Boulton to manufacture his engines. This engine was designed and built under Watt's personal guidance. It is one of the best examples of his engines to survive.

> ## Did You Know?
>
> The Boulton & Watt engine could lift 134,000 gallons of water per hour to a height of forty-two feet. It was used from 1796 to 1854 at the Warwick & Birmingham pumping station in Birmingham, England, to pump water for a series of locks on the Bordesley Canal.

Franklin Steam Engine

THIS QUINTESSENTIALLY AMERICAN STEAM ENGINE is the oldest American steam engine on exhibit in the Museum. By 1848, when Franklin Machine Works of Albany, New York, built this engine, the American horizontal stationary steam engine had evolved into an almost standard machine. These engines were usually designed to operate using high-pressure steam, an advancement over the earlier Watt engines. Installing even a small engine like this rather than water power made a huge difference in factory location, size, and operation—all sources of profit in the 1800s.

Steam power initially spread in the United States as a result of both adoption and adaptation of existing technologies in ships and boats. This engine is a direct descendant of the efficient and compact horizontal steam engines that had evolved to power Mississippi River steamboats. The steam engine's original paint scheme, with vibrant colors and applied decorative detail, speaks to the increasingly elevated status of steam technology as it found a firm footing in America's mills and factories.

This engine initially powered a sawmill, then several shops for the Michigan Central Railroad.

Gothic Engine and Corliss Engine

ALTHOUGH WATER STILL POWERED MOST AMERICAN INDUSTRIES in the mid-1800s, a sizable number of steam engines were making their appearance. Steam power gave industrialists the flexibility to place their factories anywhere—usually closer to markets for their products and within easy reach of cheap immigrant labor in the cities.

Although this particular Gothic engine was located deep inside a factory, its decorative appearance demonstrates Americans' desire at the time to harmonize unfamiliar new technologies within a familiar

LOOK CLOSER

Ornamental details on the Gothic engine—simulating those on public buildings of the Gothic Revival style—include vertical pointed arches topped by ornamental finials and quatrefoil motifs that look like four-leaf clovers.

This Gothic-style steam engine, made about 1855, powered machinery in a Philadelphia, Pennsylvania, factory.

man-made environment. It incorporates features reminiscent of the then-popular Gothic Revival style in buildings and furniture. Inspired by medieval European castles and churches, this style conveyed dignity and respectability and was intended to elicit awe and reverence.

George Corliss made the most significant contributions to American steam engine design at the time. His engines ran more efficiently than other steam engines, saving fuel. Corliss engines were powerful enough to drive many machines at once. Their smooth-running speed and swift response to changes in load also provided a great boon to the emerging textile industry in New England—both increasing production and lowering the likelihood that the delicate threads would break.

Corliss, a self-taught genius from Rhode Island, was hailed as the greatest mechanical engineer of his day. This is the only extant engine built by Corliss's own company during his lifetime.

This 1859 Corliss engine provided centralized power to several independent workshops in Providence, Rhode Island.

Highland Park Engine

THIS COLOSSAL ENGINE, built in 1916, helped power Ford Motor Company's Highland Park Plant—one of the largest and most famous factories in the world. In 1913, Model Ts were assembled here at an average of one car every forty seconds.

A huge amount of electrical power was needed to drive the thousands of machines that produced Model Ts. This led to the creation of nine combined steam and internal combustion engines. These engines, designed by and unique

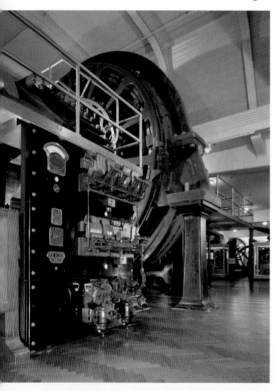

to Ford Motor Company, were a response to the limited water supply that didn't allow for the use of the more efficient and compact steam turbines that were commonly used in factories at the time.

By 1919, these nine units generating electricity for the factory, plus several massive pumps and compressors, were all on public view in a powerhouse on Woodward Avenue. Although this engine was an outmoded technology at the time, it epitomizes Henry Ford's love of steam power and his penchant for developing high-functioning, interdependent systems within his own self-sufficient factory operations.

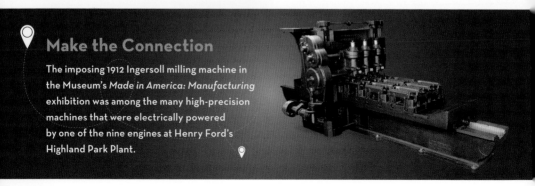

Make the Connection

The imposing 1912 Ingersoll milling machine in the Museum's *Made in America: Manufacturing* exhibition was among the many high-precision machines that were electrically powered by one of the nine engines at Henry Ford's Highland Park Plant.

Spokane Water Turbine

THIS 1903 WATER TURBINE represents the use of large-scale units for harnessing the energy of fast-running water. These units supplied electrical power that could be transmitted over long distances. The scale of electric-station power sources had become enormous by the first decade of the 1900s. This water turbine, located in Spokane, Washington, initially generated electricity to run lights and elevators in the silver mining towns of western Idaho about one hundred miles away. Over the years, such power lines were joined together into one massive network serving the entire country. This generator was decommissioned in 1990, when it became part of the *Made in America: Power* exhibition.

Large, central hydroelectric plants were very economical to run. This water turbine generator had a combined efficiency of about 85 percent, meaning that 85 percent of the energy available from the falling water was converted into electrical energy. Both the turbine portion of this machine and its generator were undoubtedly designed and built by teams of engineers.

Past *Forward*

Today, electric power generation is a national interdependent system, giving rise to the phrase "on the grid." Since this water turbine first went into operation, energy sources such as petroleum, natural gas, coal, and nuclear have been used. People are now experimenting with renewable resources like wind, solar, geothermal, hydrogen, tidal waves, and biomass energy.

Photovoltaic (solar) panels on the Visitor Center roof at the Ford Rouge Factory Tour

Enoch Ambler's patented mower, circa 1836, is thought to be the oldest surviving harvester in existence today.

Agriculture and the Environment

Farming practices are rooted in tradition. For generations, farmers tended to use the tools and techniques of their ancestors. But the special challenges American farmers faced—deep forests, dense prairie soil, new types of crops, worker shortages, and limited means of transportation—encouraged more progressive farmers to seek faster and more efficient ways of doing things. Often, improvements were small. Farmers, mechanics, and industrialists variously tried their hand at addressing these challenges with practical solutions. New inventions built upon the successes of older ones.

Mechanized operations slowly replaced tedious hand tasks, using equipment powered by animals or steam and later by internal combustion engines. Occasionally an invention would have such far-reaching impact that it would revolutionize how work was done and how much farmers could produce. These innovations not only changed farm work but also transformed people's lives. A selection of these from the Museum's *Agriculture* exhibition are highlighted here.

Workers load hay with the help of a Fordson tractor, Ford Farms, 1917.

Superior grain drill, made in Springfield, Ohio, about 1900

Innovations in Planting

PLOWS, AMONG THE OLDEST AGRICULTURAL TOOLS, broke up old growth and weeds to expose fresh soil for planting. In 1869, iron foundry owner James Oliver patented a process for hardening cast iron to make a smoother moldboard (the curved metal blade that turns the earth over), which reduced the effort the horses needed to pull the plow. A small plow at the front cut and turned the sod, while a gauge wheel regulated the depth of plowing.

The grain drill accomplished multiple steps quickly and efficiently, presenting a vast improvement over hand sowing. It distributed seeds uniformly at a controlled depth, then covered them immediately so they would not be lost to wind and birds. To make smaller furrows, the Superior grain drill replaced the less efficient shovels of earlier grain drills with discs. These discs easily cut through debris and displaced less dirt. Then the grain drill covered and fertilized the seed.

James Oliver's patented chilled plow, circa 1890

No-till planter, Deere & Company, Moline, Illinois, 1978

The 1978 Deere & Company no-till planter is the first commercially success-ful planter of its type, a significant innovation that is still used today. The no-till planter places the crop seeds directly into the soil through the residue of the previ-ous year's crop without the need for tilling, or exposing fresh soil through plowing or harrowing. This planting method, which draws heavily on the use of chemical herbicides, also prevents erosion and conserves water for crop use.

Make the Connection

The Soybean Lab Agricultural Gallery in Greenfield Village houses agricultural equipment from The Henry Ford's collection, ranging from traditional forms to innovative designs. The display includes plows, harrows, cultivators, and other tools and implements for planting.

Left: Thresher-separator, made by Westinghouse & Co., about 1870; right: Ambler's patented mowing machine, made about 1836

Innovations in Harvesting

THE MECHANICAL MOWER cut hay for livestock feed with much greater efficiency than a hand scythe. While not the first harvesting machine to be invented, Ambler's patented mowing machine is probably the oldest harvester in existence today. Enoch Ambler received a patent for a "machine for cutting grass or grain by horse power" in 1834. The horse-drawn mowing machine in the Museum's collection, based upon Ambler's patent, was made about 1836.

Massey-Harris Model 20 combine, 1938

The threshing machine replaced the hand flail—a device for knocking the grain off the straw. The combined thresher-separator, which was horse-drawn to the work site, efficiently separated the straw from both the grain and the chaff, or waste. The Westinghouse machine in the Museum's collection, made about 1870, separated the grain and tossed away the straw using an agitating or vibrating motion. Although other methods were tried, this became the universally accepted method of grain and straw separation.

The self-propelled Massey-Harris Model 20 combine, introduced in 1938, embodied over one hundred years of improvements in mechanical harvesters. It accomplished all grain harvesting tasks in a single operation—cutting grain, separating out and carrying away the straw, and binding the wheat. It could be maneuvered over different kinds of terrain, required only one operator, reduced costs from previous machines, and eliminated grain loss. With the self-propelled combine, the annual communitywide grain harvest became a solitary task undertaken by one person.

LOOK CLOSER

In the Museum's *Agriculture* exhibition, visitors can climb up inside the cab of another combine—the 1975 Sperry-New Holland TR70—and imagine what it was like for farmers to harvest crops using such a massive machine.

Sperry-New Holland combine, 1975

Tractors for the Small Farmer

HENRY FORD DEVOTED a great deal of effort to improving farmers' lives through mechanization. Beginning about 1906, Ford directed his engineers

to devise a tractor to replace the horse on the farm. At the time, most tractors weighed more than two tons and cost around $1,000. Ford hoped to create a small, inexpensive tractor that most farmers could afford. After years of experimentation, he introduced the Fordson tractor. This "Model T" of farm power, introduced in 1917, was mass-produced and inexpensive, and it rapidly became the most popular tractor in the United States.

1917 Fordson tractor, given to agriculturist Luther Burbank by Henry Ford

Unfortunately, the Fordson tractor could only be used with a limited number of implements. In October 1938, Harry Ferguson demonstrated to Henry Ford his innovative "three-point hitch" hydraulic system, which created a smoother interaction between the tractor and the implement and helped surmount the Fordson's limits. Ford was so impressed that the two men went into partnership. Their efforts resulted in this 1939 prototype and a popular eight-year production run.

Harry Ferguson and Henry Ford with Model 9N tractor, 1939

Make the Connection

Before tractors, portable horse-drawn agricultural steam engines powered large farm equipment. Young Henry Ford operated a Westinghouse portable steam engine, now in the *Agriculture* exhibition, for a threshing crew, later claiming that it inspired his confidence in working with machines.

Henry Ford (right) with the Westinghouse steam engine, 1920

Rust Cotton Picker and Tomato Harvester

INNOVATIONS CAN IMPACT PEOPLE IN DIFFERENT WAYS. The Rust cotton picker was the first commercially successful self-propelled machine for picking cotton—the last major American crop to be mechanized. Self-taught inventor John Daniel Rust, assisted by his mechanical engineering brother Mack, developed a machine that could pick the equivalent amount of cotton in one day as seventy-five to one hundred workers. While saving labor, this machine also put millions of southern African American farm laborers out of work, contributing to their mass migration to northern cities during the 1950s.

Around the same time, plant scientist Jack Hanna and agricultural engineer Coby Lorenzen teamed up at the University of California-Davis to invent a machine that could mechanically harvest tomatoes. Their efforts resulted in

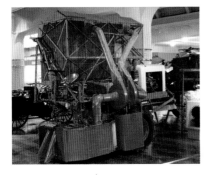

Rust cotton picker, made in Pine Bluff, Arkansas, 1950

not only a machine that successfully accomplished this, but also a genetically modified tomato that was tough and could be easily destemmed during harvesting. Using the tomato harvester, large agribusinesses increased output, doubling the California tomato industry, while many small farmers were pushed out of the tomato processing business.

Past *Forward*

The tomato harvester not only encouraged agribusiness, but ironically it also led to renewed small-scale farming. When thousands of farm workers lost their jobs because of this machine, a varied coalition of activists defending the rights of small farmers brought about legal battles that resulted in new initiatives to support sustainable and alternative farming practices.

FMC tomato harvester, made in San Jose, California, 1969

The Apple 1, from 1976, was the first personal computer that allowed people to type on a keyboard and then display that text on a monitor.

Design and Making Things

The Industrial Revolution in America—particularly the period from about 1820 to 1920—radically altered how things were made and how workers did their jobs. The multitude of innovations that evolved at that time laid the foundation for how Americans live and work today.

With so many new products becoming available from the late 1800s through the first half of the 1900s, manufacturers depended upon advertisers and then industrial designers to both stimulate consumer demand and ensure that their products would stand out over those of their competitors. By the 1950s, industrial design had come to imply more than the aesthetic refinement of consumer products. Deeply influenced by the work and philosophy of designers such as Charles and Ray Eames, industrial design became centered around the idea of problem solving. It was seen as a way to improve the quality of people's lives while advancing human knowledge and understanding.

This section highlights innovative processes and products from several Museum exhibitions: *Made in America: Manufacturing, Clockwork, Fully Furnished, Mathematica,* the Dymaxion House, and the Davidson-Gerson Modern Glass Gallery.

From a Herman Miller, Inc., postcard advertising "Chairs by Charles Eames," 1951–65

41

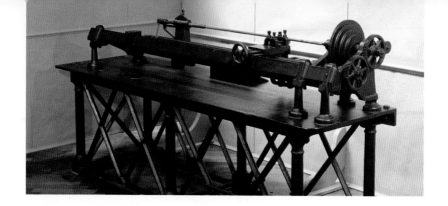

Maudslay Production Lathe

After the Revolutionary War, many Americans claimed that their new nation was self-reliant. But, in reality, a great deal of technical knowledge, monetary capital, and skilled labor came from Europe. One of the most important achievements of the early Industrial Revolution was the ability to cut metal with extreme accuracy—and imported knowledge, capital, and labor were all crucial to the development of these precision machine tools. In fact, later products like clocks, sewing machines, and automobiles would not have been possible without the development of machines like these.

British machinist Henry Maudslay is generally credited with developing the first truly satisfactory lathes for accurately machining metal and cutting metal screw threads. Maudslay's perfectionism resulted in tools and engines that achieved unprecedented standards. His London-based factory was also a training ground for young machine-tool builders who went on to develop machines that achieved even higher levels of precision. This Maudslay production lathe, made about 1804, is thought to be the earliest surviving industrial-capacity precision machine tool in the world.

Make the Connection

Maudslay's lathe laid the foundation for later precision metal-cutting lathes in machine shops like the one Henry Ford worked in as a young man. Armington & Sims, a generalized re-creation of such a machine shop, is in Greenfield Village.

Blanchard Wood-Copying Lathe

PERHAPS THE MOST ORIGINAL MACHINE TOOL to emerge in the United States before 1830 was the gunstock-duplicating machine of Thomas Blanchard. A Mas-

sachusetts machinist with a natural inventive streak, Blanchard became convinced that he could develop a lathe for turning out multiple copies of irregularly shaped wooden gunstocks. The resulting invention, patented in 1819, caught the attention of government officials at the Springfield (Massachusetts) Armory—the primary center for manufacturing United States military firearms since 1777. On contract with the armory, Blanchard and his assistants eventually created a series of machines that mechanized all the steps in gunstock production.

This duplicating lathe, from about 1865, used Blanchard's patents as its basis. It made copies using a rotating blade whose position was guided by the shape of the initial prototype, or master pattern. These lathes—readily operated by semi-skilled workers—could shape such irregular wooden objects as ax handles, shoe lasts (wooden forms shaped like feet for manufacturing or repairing shoes), or rifle stocks in about ten minutes.

Did You Know?

Like other inventors, Thomas Blanchard took advantage of the American patent system, which ensured exclusive rights to inventions for a set amount of time. This government-regulated system greatly encouraged individual ingenuity and enterprise.

Mass Production at Highland Park

NO OBJECT IS MORE EMBLEMATIC of America's Industrial Revolution than the Model T. To meet high demand, Henry Ford and his assistants perfected a system of mass production that reduced the time of producing Model Ts from about twelve-and-one-half man-hours to only one-and-one-half man-hours.

There were more than ten thousand parts in a Model T. Henry Ford's moving assembly line required that each one of these parts be manufactured to exacting tolerances (their acceptable amount of variation) and be fully interchangeable with any other part of its kind. By organizing the automobile's construction into a series of distinct small steps and using precision machinery, the assembly line generated enormous gains in productivity.

Machines like this 1912 Ingersoll milling machine—capable of undertaking highly accurate, multiple cutting operations on many components at the same time—were crucial to the high production levels attained at the Highland Park factory. This machine is the only survivor of the vast range of custom-designed high-production machine tools used at Highland Park.

1912 Ingersoll milling machine

Make the Connection

The "exploded" Model T at the entrance to *Made in America: Manufacturing* dramatizes the numerous parts that went into making Model Ts, while the hands-on Build a Model T program offers visitors the opportunity to assemble a Model T from various components.

"Exploded" Model T

Early Clocks

CLOCKS WERE ONE OF THE EARLIEST CONSUMER GOODS made with standardized parts and produced in quantity. For centuries, their inner mechanisms had been laboriously shaped by hand.

During the first decade of the 1800s, Connecticut clock maker Eli Terry simplified the construction methods for producing wooden clock movements (the

Eli Terry clock movement, 1808-09

timekeeping mechanisms inside the clocks). Two decades later, he developed the compact "pillar and scroll" shelf clock, making these in such quantity that many more people could afford clocks than ever before. Then he tapped into the growing market for clocks by sending out traveling Yankee peddlers to sell them door-to-door. Many clock makers would follow Terry's innovative leads.

During the late 1830s, brothers Chauncey and Noble Jerome developed a brass clock movement that could be mass-produced with uniform parts. Using dies to stamp out clock movements from sheet brass, their shelf clocks were even more reliable and affordable than the earlier wood-movement clocks of Eli Terry and other clock makers. Soon, it seemed, everyone owned a shelf clock.

LOOK CLOSER

Terry's shelf clocks became known as "pillar and scroll" because of the two side pillars and the scrolled woodwork on top. Jerome shelf clocks were later called "ogee" because of the S-shaped molding around their frames, simulating furniture forms.

"Pillar and scroll"-type shelf clock, made by Eli Terry, 1817-21

Practical Innovations for the Home

TODAY, PEOPLE ASSUME that new labor-saving devices were always immediately accepted into the home. But this was often not the case.

Sewing machines came on the market in the 1850s, but they were initially used in shops to produce men's ready-made clothing. They were not embraced for home use because they were expensive and because operating machines was considered unfeminine. Elegantly dressed women

Florence sewing machine, 1860–65

demonstrating sewing machines in showrooms led to wider acceptance, as did lower costs. In the twentieth century, the ready-made clothing industry would turn home sewing into a mere hobby.

Michigan Stove Company cookstove, made about 1890

The cast-iron cookstove, introduced in the 1830s, was undoubtedly the most important cooking innovation of the 1800s. Wood- and coal-burning stoves promised to reduce the hazards of fireplace cooking, cook food more evenly, and eliminate the tedious stooping and heavy lifting of cookware. In addition, they burned less fuel than the open fireplace. It took decades, however, for many women to switch to this entirely new way of cooking because they insisted that food cooked over the open fire tasted better. These stoves were also expensive and often performed poorly.

1930s kitchen setting in Museum with General Electric Monitor Top refrigerator

During the 1920s, manufacturers began a massive campaign to convince homeowners of the wonders of electric refrigeration. But they were considered a luxury item compared with the popular icebox, and low-cost electrical power was not widely available yet. General Electric's monthly payment plan made its Monitor Top model one of the first truly popular electric refrigerators.

Past *Forward*

Innovations for the home continued to be developed and have a major impact on people's lives. Cleaner, more dependable gas and electric ranges replaced coal-burning cookstoves, especially after automatic thermostats were introduced in the 1920s. Electric refrigerators encouraged people to eat fresher, more varied foods, while increasingly larger freezer compartments added convenience.

1929 Frigidaire ad

47

The Dymaxion House

R. BUCKMINSTER FULLER WAS A PHILOSOPHER, inventor, and designer best known for his invention of the geodesic dome. The Dymaxion House, conceived in the late 1920s, was Fuller's attempt to look at the house as a whole system. Rather than following the traditional process of architects and house builders, he approached the problem of designing an affordable and efficient house in a new way. He used a scientific (often mathematical) process to analyze human needs, then applied technological solutions to address these needs.

By the mid-1940s, technology had caught up with Fuller's ideas in the form of malleable aluminum and high-strength aluminum alloys that had been developed in the wartime aviation industry. The timing seemed right to produce these houses, keeping wartime aircraft workers in jobs while addressing the postwar housing shortage.

Buckminster Fuller in *Fortune* magazine, 1946

Fuller convinced Beech Aircraft of Wichita, Kansas, to help bring his Dymaxion House to fruition—a house that would cost about $6,500 in 1946 (approximately the price of a high-end automobile). The house would be shipped in parts inside a steel container to the home-owner's desired location, and, when assem-bled, be suspended from a central column. Hundreds of potential homeowners expressed interest. But as costs for retooling the factory grew and disagreements between Fuller and his investors multiplied, the project was shelved. Meanwhile, the wartime ban on standard housing materials was lifted, and Americans found comfort in returning to traditional housing styles.

Did You Know?

Fuller Houses, Inc., estimated that the 1,017-square-foot Dymaxion House would weigh about four tons, while a typical house of the era, constructed of wood and other traditional materials, weighed approximately 150 tons.

Hitchcock Side Chair

FURNITURE MAKING HAD A LONG TRADITION of hand craftsmanship. Individual pieces—made to order—were low in production numbers and relatively high in cost. But Lambert Hitchcock had another idea. Inspired by the bustling firearms and clock industries in his home state of Connecticut, he dreamed of manufacturing affordable chairs by using machine-made interchangeable parts that were easy to produce and assemble.

In 1818, Hitchcock built a factory at the confluence of two fast-moving rivers in northwestern Connecticut. Soon, he was turning out some fifteen thousand chairs per year at prices ranging from $0.45 to $1.75.

In 1825, Hitchcock went even further by organizing his factory into the separate steps needed to manufacture, assemble, and decorate chairs. He opened retail stores, sold chairs wholesale, and distributed chairs through the same network of traveling Yankee peddlers that Eli Terry had used to sell his clocks.

Hitchcock's chairs became so popular that many competitors tried to imitate them. To this day, chairs of this style are referred to as Hitchcock chairs.

Chair made at Hitchcock Chair Factory, Riverton, Connecticut, 1825–35

Changing Ideals of Comfort

AT FIRST, CHAIRS THAT WERE PHYSICALLY COMFORTABLE were hidden from public view, used only by the elderly, invalids, or nursing mothers. But the invention of coiled-iron springs and machine-produced upholstery ushered in a new era of "stuffed" furniture. By the 1880s, upholstered platform rockers appeared in many parlors across the country, combining fashion on the outside with innovative rocking mechanisms on the inside.

Platform rocker, 1885–95

The La-Z-Boy Reclina Rocker embodied a newer ideal of comfort. During the early 1900s, the living room replaced the formal parlor as the public room of the house. In contrast to the staid and formal furnishings of the Victorian parlor, living room furnishings were intended for family relaxation. Springs, upholstery, rocker, recliner, and patented mechanisms all converged and entered the family living room in the form of upholstered recliners—epitomized by the La-Z-Boy chair. The 1961 Reclina Rocker boosted La-Z-Boy sales from $1.1 million in 1961 to $52.7 million in 1971.

La-Z-Boy Reclina Rocker, 1961

Did You Know?

Two enterprising cousins—Edward M. Knabusch and Edwin J. Shoemaker—founded the La-Z-Boy Company in Monroe, Michigan, in 1928. Their first product was an adjustable slatted-wood porch chair. Springs, upholstery, and built-in ottomans would come later.

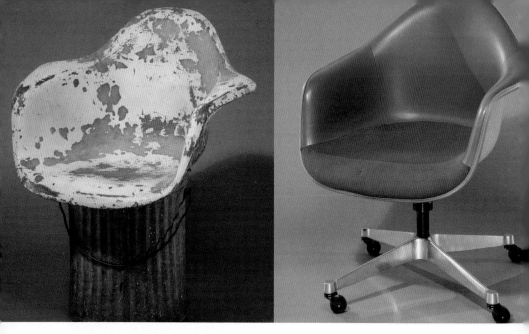

Left: John Wills fiberglass armchair, made about 1949; right: molded fiberglass armchair on swivel base, 1954-65

The Furniture of Charles and Ray Eames

THE INNOVATIVE WORK OF CHARLES AND RAY EAMES has strongly influenced modern society's understanding of the design process and the role of the designer. Charles Eames and his wife, Ray, aimed to use new materials and industrial processes to produce high-quality, everyday objects at affordable prices.

The fiberglass chair shell perched on the trash can represents an early step in the lengthy design and production process for the Eames fiberglass-reinforced plastic chair. Charles had sought out the skills of boatbuilder John Wills, known for developing a fiberglass-plastic formula that could harden at room temperature without the use of pressure. Wills ultimately produced two prototype chairs, each of which he expediently raised to a convenient sitting height on makeshift trash can bases so Charles could test them out. Charles purchased one; this is the other chair, the one that remained in Wills's shop for almost fifty years. The development and refinement of this design continued, leading to highly successful variants produced by Herman Miller, Inc.

The iconic Eames lounge chair and ottoman, introduced in 1956 and manufactured by Herman Miller, Inc., was intended to be a lighter, more elegant,

Detail from a poster advertising the 1976 Herman Miller, Inc., exhibit *Connections: The Work of Charles and Ray Eames*

modern-looking version of the conventional, ponderous English club chair. Charles felt that the lounge chair should have the warm receptive look of a well-used first baseman's mitt. After a long, intricate development process, the final result combined a curved rosewood shell with plush upholstered leather on an aluminum swivel base.

Eames lounge chair and ottoman, introduced 1956

Aeron Chair
Pre-Production Prototype

THE IDEA OF DESIGNING products based upon the scientific study of human factors, or ergonomics, expanded during the second half of the 1900s—particularly as people interacted with computers and keyboards.

The ergonomic Aeron chair had its origins in the 1980s, when Herman Miller, Inc., asked designers Bill Stumpf and Don Chadwick to investigate ways to create better furniture for the elderly. Stumpf and Chadwick completed their first prototype, called the Sarah chair, in 1988. This chair's many innovations included a span of breathable plastic fabric that stretched across its frame underneath a foam cushion.

The Sarah chair was never produced, but Herman Miller asked Stumpf and Chadwick if they could apply what they learned to an office chair. They scrapped the foam cushion but kept the breathable mesh fabric, which had the added advantages of being environmentally friendly and economical to produce. The Aeron chair, introduced in 1994, appealed to some because of its high-design look but, for most people, its biggest selling point was that it was incredibly comfortable.

Aeron task chair prototype, 1994

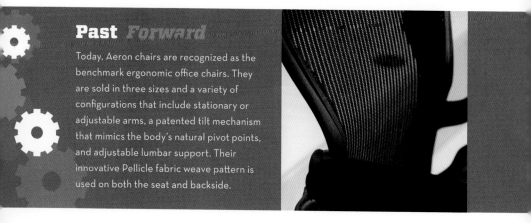

Past *Forward*

Today, Aeron chairs are recognized as the benchmark ergonomic office chairs. They are sold in three sizes and a variety of configurations that include stationary or adjustable arms, a patented tilt mechanism that mimics the body's natural pivot points, and adjustable lumbar support. Their innovative Pellicle fabric weave pattern is used on both the seat and backside.

Telephones

FROM ALEXANDER GRAHAM BELL'S first experiments in 1876, telephones have become vital to social and business life in America. The three telephones highlighted here show the varied ways in which innovation can occur.

Did You Know?

Almon Strowger, the inventor of the Strowger switch for the potbelly desk stand telephone, was an undertaker in Kansas City, Missouri. He developed this switch because the phone operators in town kept putting business through to his competition.

The potbelly desk stand telephone, from around 1890, was the first dial telephone. Almon Strowger's switching mechanism allowed people to dial one another directly.

Western Electric's 300 Series telephones were the company's first self-contained phones, incorporating the handset, dial, and bells into a compact integrated unit. The popular Model 302 phone, designed in 1937 by the firm of renowned industrial designer Henry Dreyfuss, was produced with only slight variations until 1954.

Telephone with Strowger switch, circa 1890

The iPhone marks the culmination of the cell phone as a pocket computer. This handheld device is a telephone, music player, television, and Internet-enabled device in one, with a trendsetting touchscreen interface. When the iPhone was released in 2007, buyers waited in lines for hours at Apple stores across the country.

Apple iPhone, 2007

Western Electric 300 Series telephone, 1937

Original *Mathematica* exhibit at the California Museum of Science and Industry, Los Angeles

Mathematica

CHARLES AND RAY EAMES were fascinated by the power of images to inform, entertain, persuade, and trigger emotional responses. Beginning in the late 1950s, their Venice, California–based office—which included a staff of talented designers and developers—produced a growing body of media pieces, exhibitions, and

"Multiplication Cube" in *Mathematica* exhibit

books. Perhaps the most famous of these is their 1961 exhibition *Mathematica: A World of Numbers ... and Beyond.* Originally funded by IBM, *Mathematica* is the first interactive exhibition devoted to math. Charles and Ray's intent was to reveal the genuine fun of math and science to the broadest possible audience—to, as Charles put it, "let the cat out of the bag."

While it showcases compelling artifacts of mathematical exploration, *Mathematica* itself is an artifact. It was the first major exhibition that the Eames Office produced, a three-thousand-square-foot expression that opened

in March 1961 in the new science wing of the California Museum of Science and Industry (and later moved to the New York Hall of Science). After the success of the first *Mathematica*, second and third variants were produced. The second variant opened at the Chicago Museum of Science and Industry, then moved to the Boston Museum of Science. The third variant, created for the IBM Pavilion at the 1964–65 New York World's Fair, is the one that The Henry Ford acquired in 2014.

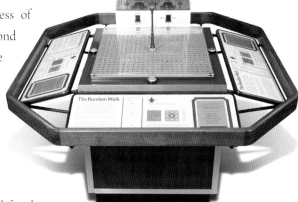

"Random Walk"

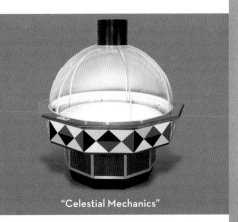

"Celestial Mechanics"

Apple 1 Computer

On March 5, 1975, some of the most radical minds in computing met for the inaugural meeting of the Homebrew Computer Club, an early computer hobbyist group in Silicon Valley. Steve Wozniak, then an engineer working at Hewlett-Packard, attended this meeting and walked away inspired to create an affordable and powerful computer for the everyday home user.

Using the new 6502 MOS microprocessor chip, Wozniak condensed his design onto a small rectangular circuit board holding sixty chips. He also gave some thought to a user-friendly interface and "hassle-free" initial setup. The Apple 1 is the first personal computer that allowed people to type on a keyboard and have their text show up on a television monitor. It also came preassembled rather than in the usual kit form that was common for computers in the 1970s.

In 1976, Wozniak's engineering skills, coupled with his friend Steve Jobs's bold marketing moves, led to their first Apple 1 order—from Byte Shop owner Paul Terrell for two hundred assembled motherboards.

MACWORLD

Premier issue of *MACWORLD*, 1984

Davidson-Gerson Modern Glass Gallery

THE DAVIDSON-GERSON MODERN GLASS GALLERY—a blend of art, science, and technological innovation—embraces the notion of glass as a medium for artistic expression, in contrast to its use in industrial production.

The studio glass movement was born in 1962, when American teaching ceramist Harvey Littleton held two historic glassblowing workshops at the Toledo Museum of Art to explore ways that artists might create works of glass art in their own studios. Glass research scientist Dominick Labino contributed advice on the design of small, inexpensive portable furnaces in which glass could be melted and worked. He also supplied glass that could be melted at a lower temperature than industrial glass.

With Littleton's active encouragement and promotion, glass programs sprang up at universities, art schools, and workshops across the country during the 1960s and early 1970s. Studio glass artists like Dale Chihuly and Marvin Lipofsky played seminal roles in raising awareness worldwide. Successive generations of artists have shared technical knowledge and ideas and taken glassblowing in a myriad of experimental and innovative directions.

Yellow Chiffon Venetian Ikebana with Putti and Prunts by Dale Chihuly, 2002

December Song by Jon Kuhn, 2000

Make the Connection

In the Greenfield Village Glass Shop, skilled artisans demonstrate glass production techniques from the earliest days into the 1900s. Adjacent to the shop is the Davidson-Gerson Gallery of Glass that shows the interaction between American glass and American culture over 350 years.

The 1965 Ford Mustang—sporty, stylish, and roomy—became an unprecedented success story by tapping into the new youth market.

Mobility

Americans have long been characterized as a people on the move—crossing the vast continent, pursuing new opportunities, and reinventing themselves under new circumstances. To achieve these ends, they have developed a range of transportation vehicles—from sturdy horse-drawn carriages to powerful locomotives, from reliable automobiles to seemingly miraculous flying machines. Many of these were small steps in a larger evolution; others were innovations with major impact. Experimentation and innovation continue today with changing trends in personal and shared mobility and in mass transit.

The Museum's railroad collection shows how different locomotives and railcars transformed people's lives. The *Driving America* exhibition showcases the Museum's significant automobiles and explores themes like the impact of cars on the environment, safety, and road developments. Five stately presidential vehicles are displayed here, along with a significant collection of race cars that tested the limits of speed, durability, endurance, control, and power. The *Heroes of the Sky: Adventures in Early Flight* exhibition recounts the stories of adventurous barnstormers, inventors, explorers, record breakers, and entrepreneurs who laid the foundations for dramatic aviation innovations to come.

Concord coach with passengers, about 1885

Abbot-Downing Concord Coach

FOREIGN VISITORS TO THE UNITED STATES during the 1800s often remarked that Americans always seemed to be in a hurry. Indeed, from early on, vehicles were developed that seemed to align with this character trait: unique American vehicles of light, strong construction; fast speed; and freedom of movement.

Until the coming of the railroad in the mid- and late 1800s, traveling long distances usually meant riding in public stagecoaches. An elaborate network of routes for carrying mail, freight, and passengers connected cities and towns. J. Stephens Abbot and Lewis Downing of Concord, New Hampshire, created the Concord coach, one of the most significant horse-drawn vehicles developed in America. First built in the late 1820s, the Concord coach featured an innovative suspension system that supported the coach body on thick leather straps called thoroughbraces. The rocking motion this produced was easier on both passengers and horses traveling over rough roads. Abbot-Downing not only shipped its coaches West, but the company also exported them to Australia, South Africa, and South America.

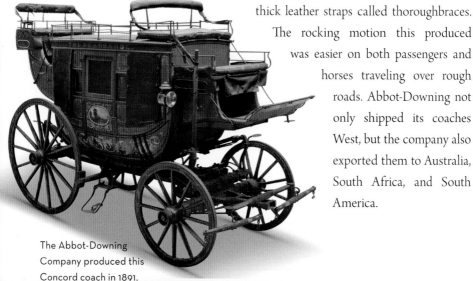

The Abbot-Downing Company produced this Concord coach in 1891.

Make the Connection

Greenfield Village visitors can see what it's like to ride in a horse-drawn vehicle—aboard a horse-drawn omnibus like those from the 1800s and in horse-drawn wagons during Holiday Nights. Wedding guests can also ride in special horse-drawn carriages.

Jones Horse-Drawn Streetcar

LIVING IN THE CITY brought unique transportation needs. Various modes of transportation were developed to ease congestion and move large numbers of people from place to place.

The horse-drawn streetcar, or horsecar, was a significant innovation. It sported iron wheels and ran on iron rails, making an easier pull for horses and a smoother ride for passengers than the earlier horse-drawn omnibuses that traveled over bumpy roads. The first horsecars went into service in New York City in 1832. By the late 1880s, some eighteen thousand horsecars operated over four hundred street railways in the United States.

Horsecars operating over street railways allowed people to move farther from their workplace, facilitating the growth of suburbs. This horsecar is a small one, intended to carry only fifteen passengers and be pulled by a single horse. Built around 1875, it was used by the Brooklyn City Railroad between 1881 and 1897—about the time that larger electric streetcars were becoming popular. Within a few decades, motorized buses would replace all streetcars.

LOOK CLOSER

This streetcar is double-ended, which allowed it to operate in either direction after the horse was moved accordingly. The wording across the top, "Hunters Point & Erie Basin," refers to this streetcar's run from Hunters Point in Long Island City, Queens, to Erie Basin in South Brooklyn.

Fruit Growers Express Refrigerator Car

RAILROAD REFRIGERATOR CARS revolutionized meatpacking and other agricultural industries by tremendously broadening the markets to which fresh produce could be delivered. Experimentation with various designs for ice-cooled refrigerator cars began in the 1860s. By the time this car was built in 1924, some 150,000 such cars were in use.

This car was built and operated by Fruit Growers Express Company of Alexandria, Virginia, a pioneer in refrigerator car service. Blocks of ice were loaded through roof hatches into large bunkers at each end of the car. Fans, driven by the car's axles, helped to circulate the cool air. Insulation was provided by dry air

trapped in fibrous material (such as mats of felted flax or cattle hair), sandwiched into the car's floor and walls. Despite this clever design, ice melted quickly in these refrigerator cars. So a national network of company-owned ice-making and ice-loading installations was developed to continually supply ice to the cars.

Past *Forward*

Refrigerator cars allowed regions with extended growing seasons, such as Florida and California, to market their produce across the country—greatly expanding their industries while allowing people in cold climates to enjoy fresh fruits and vegetables year-round. After World War II, mechanically cooled refrigerator trucks began to replace rail for transporting perishable goods.

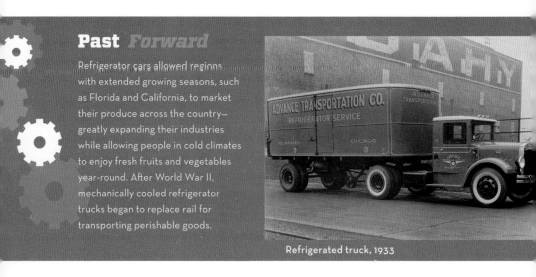

Refrigerated truck, 1933

Allegheny Steam Locomotive

THE CHESAPEAKE & OHIO RAILWAY's Allegheny locomotives, introduced in 1941, represented the peak of steam locomotive technology. Among the largest and most powerful steam locomotives ever built, they could generate 7,500 horsepower. The Allegheny was the culmination of refinements made by mechanical engineer William Woodard at the Lima Locomotive Works, Inc., in Ohio. Woodard's rigorous and systematic approach emphasized increased heating area and the efficient use of high-pressure, high-temperature steam.

LOOK CLOSER

Alongside the Museum's Allegheny, visitors can press buttons to hear what the locomotive's bell and whistle sounded like. They can also climb inside the cab to imagine what it was like for the Allegheny's crew to operate this 389-ton locomotive.

While the Allegheny was capable of hauling trains at speeds of up to seventy miles per hour, this type of locomotive more often worked at lower speeds

hauling freight—mostly coal—over the Allegheny Mountains in trains that were often a mile and a quarter in length. During World War II, these locomotives were put into service hauling military troops, wounded soldiers, and prisoners of war. Although the Allegheny's steam technology was highly advanced, it was no match for the more economical diesel locomotives. Just eleven years after introducing them, the Chesapeake & Ohio began pulling these giants from service.

This Allegheny steam locomotive was produced in 1941.

1896 Quadricycle

Henry Ford and the Model T

PERHAPS MORE THAN ANY OTHER innovation of the 1900s, the Ford Model T changed the way Americans lived.

In the 1890s, nobody knew what a successful car should look like. Across Europe and America, inventors were building horseless carriages in shops, sheds,

and garages. Henry Ford was an active member of Detroit's horseless-carriage community. He read technical magazines and worked on automobiles in his spare time with mechanically inclined friends. Ford's first car, the Quadricycle, was built with off-the-shelf parts and standard machine tools. He chose a gasoline-burning internal combustion engine to power it.

Left: Henry Ford driving his Quadricycle in Detroit, 1896; right: Ford achieved a breakthrough with this experimental gasoline engine in 1893, often referred to as the "Kitchen Sink Engine."

1914 Ford Model T

After two failed companies, Ford finally succeeded with Ford Motor Company in 1903. Ford's vision from the beginning was to build an affordable "motor-car for the great multitude." His company produced a series of both large and small models. Then, working with a handpicked team of his most talented people, he introduced his dream car, the Model T, on October 1, 1908. It combined light weight with strength, power, flexibility, and ease of use—all for only $850. By 1922, with the help of the moving assembly line, a Model T could be purchased for less than $300.

The Ford Model T became a phenomenon in the United States and worldwide. People drove the cars everywhere, using them for work and pleasure, on the farm and in town. Because of the Model T, by the late 1920s most people couldn't imagine a time when there weren't cars.

Make the Connection

In The Henry Ford's Model T district of Greenfield Village, visitors can enter the re-created shed in which the Quadricycle was produced and see a scaled-down re-creation of Ford's first factory. In season, they can ride an authentic operating Model T.

Gas, Steam, or Electric?

NO SINGLE ENGINE TYPE DOMINATED the early automobile market. Cars with steam engines, electric motors, and gasoline-powered internal combustion engines all sold well.

Despite the rare boiler explosion, steam power was safe and reliable. Decades of experience with steam—in trains, boats, farms, and factories—made steam automobiles seem familiar to Americans. Water was heated to create steam by burning fuel such as kerosene, naphtha, or gasoline. But drivers needed patience. It took at least ten minutes to start an early steamer.

Electric cars were easy to drive, quiet, and dependable, but after only twenty to thirty miles, their heavy batteries were depleted and drivers had to find a charging station. Electrics were perfect for city dwellers who didn't drive far and had access to electricity. Women loved them because they started instantly without hand cranking and did not require shifting gears.

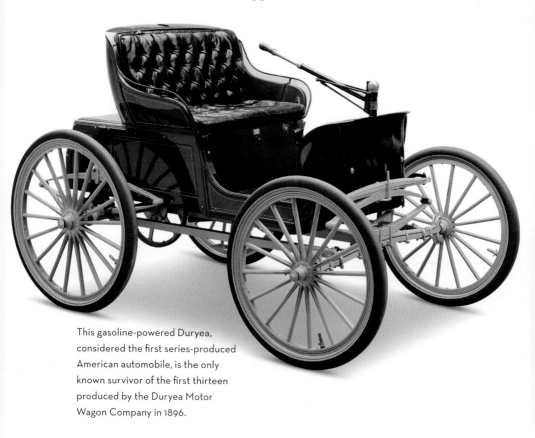

This gasoline-powered Duryea, considered the first series-produced American automobile, is the only known survivor of the first thirteen produced by the Duryea Motor Wagon Company in 1896.

Internal combustion gasoline engines were noisy, smelly, and dirty, needing frequent tinkering and regular additions of oil. To start the car, the driver had to stand in front of it and turn the engine over with a crank. There were no dedicated gas stations yet, so drivers often carried containers of gasoline with them.

Despite the disadvantages of gasoline-powered cars, their unlimited range and potential for improvement made them the dominant choice. The discovery of oil in Texas in 1901 made gasoline especially cheap and easily available.

1914 Detroit Electric, driven by Henry Ford's wife, Clara

1907 White Model G steam touring car

Past *Forward*

In the early 2000s, the threat of global warming and rising gasoline prices led to the introduction of new types of vehicles, especially hybrids and electric cars. Today, as gasoline prices fluctuate, electric power stations increase, and alternative energy sources are explored, the jury is still out on what the power/fuel source of the future will be.

1997 General Motors EV1 electric car with charging station

1927 LaSalle Roadster

THE 1927 LASALLE set a groundbreaking new direction for how automobiles were designed. Before this time, automobile manufacturers had stressed mechanical superiority. Appearance and style were generally seen as expensive features of custom-built cars. But when closed-roofed cars became the norm, people started demanding more comforts than were being offered by the trusty but bare-bones Model T.

In 1926, Alfred P. Sloan Jr., president of General Motors, saw the need for a lower-priced companion to the Cadillac to fill out the company's product line. He lured Los Angeles custom-body designer Harley Earl to Detroit for the project. The result was the 1927 LaSalle, which incorporated the radical notion of unifying the various parts of the car to enhance its overall appearance, including rounding off sharp edges and corners and lowering the car's overall silhouette. The idea of automobile "styling" for the mass market was born, setting the standard for both GM and other car companies.

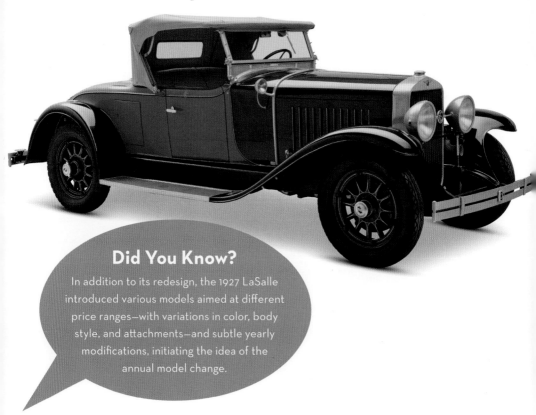

Did You Know?

In addition to its redesign, the 1927 LaSalle introduced various models aimed at different price ranges—with variations in color, body style, and attachments—and subtle yearly modifications, initiating the idea of the annual model change.

1936 Lincoln Zephyr

DURING THE 1930s, industrial designers like Raymond Loewy, Walter Dorwin Teague, and Henry Dreyfuss created a new design vocabulary, one that seemed thoroughly modern. Called streamlining, it was based upon the new science of aerodynamics. Airplanes designed in the shape of a teardrop and with aerodynamic lines actually eliminated wind resistance. They also came to symbolize motion, speed, efficiency, and progress. Streamlined design and the principles it embodied soon spread to railroads, automobiles, and a plethora of consumer products.

Since creating the Model T in 1908, Henry Ford had remained stubbornly wedded to the idea that mechanics were all that mattered in cars; design was just a frill. It was his son, Edsel, who argued for the increased prominence of style at Ford Motor Company. Edsel's efforts finally paid off with the Lincoln Zephyr. Named after the speedy Burlington Zephyr train, which had set many speed records on its run from Denver to Chicago, the Lincoln Zephyr captured both public and critical acclaim.

LOOK CLOSER

The Zephyr's design incorporates many features that reflect the influence of streamlining: its flowing teardrop shape, V-shaped front grille, headlights blending smoothly into the front fenders, rear fenders hugging the body, and fender skirts hiding the rear wheels.

1943 Willys-Overland Jeep

DURING WORLD WAR II, the ubiquitous Jeep symbolized American ingenuity and can-do determination to Allies and enemies alike. Soldiers loved the rugged little vehicle because it could go anywhere and do almost anything. They used it to tow artillery, carry the wounded, and deliver ammunition. When fitted with a machine gun, the Jeep even became a weapon.

The outbreak of war in Europe had brought a new urgency to the US Army's quest for a vehicle capable of traversing rough terrain. Requests for proposals went out to some 135 domestic automobile companies. The American Bantam Car Company submitted a prototype developed by talented freelance designer Karl Probst, promising to meet the army's tight deadline. The company received the bid, but it lacked production capacity, so the government turned to both Willys-Overland and Ford Motor Company to manufacture the Jeeps.

Jeeps of all configurations were used by many Allied powers. This particular Jeep was likely shipped to England in support of the buildup of US troops in preparation for the D-day invasion.

Past *Forward*

After World War II, surplus military Jeeps were popular—especially with returning soldiers—as were newly made civilian Jeeps. The Jeep brand appealed to customers looking for a four-wheel-drive, ultra-utilitarian vehicle. In 1984, the Jeep Cherokee became the first of a newly named class of sport utility vehicles. Chrysler acquired the Jeep brand in 1987.

1969 Jeep ad

1948 Tucker and
1949 Volkswagen Beetle

AFTER THE HARDSHIPS OF THE GREAT DEPRESSION and World War II, families pursued their dreams as never before. Home and family were top priorities, followed by buying new things. For many, cars were first on the list.

The Tucker '48 automobile was the brainchild of entrepreneur and salesman extraordinaire Preston Thomas Tucker and designed by renowned stylist Alex Tremulis. It represents one of the last attempts by an independent carmaker to break in to the high-volume car business. The car appealed to buyers not only by looking futuristic, but also by promising many new innovations for comfort, convenience, and safety. Unfortunately, Tucker's unorthodox fund-raising strategies led to bad publicity and legal trouble. Only fifty-one units were ever assembled.

The Volkswagen Beetle, first imported from Germany in 1949, recalled the spirit of Henry Ford's legendary Model T. Both cars were simple, reliable, and economical. The Beetle got more than twice the gas mileage of the average American car while costing much less. The VW would go on to break Ford's all-time sales record.

Did You Know?

After World War II, forty-hour workweeks (down from forty-four hours) and two-week paid vacations became standard in most labor union contracts. Families flooded the highways in their new cars, enjoying their paid vacations and all that America had to offer.

1948 Tucker

1949 Volkswagen Beetle

1955 Chevy Bel Air and 1960 Corvair

DURING THE 1950s, people believed things would keep getting better. After all, they were living with the benefits of the machine age—surely, improvements would continue. Even those who hadn't yet participated in the upswing hoped to do so soon.

Postwar cars were generally durable. So annual styling changes—introduced in the late 1920s—became vital to attract buyers. Stylists in the 1950s combined jet airplane shapes with exciting colors and textures, making yesterday's cars seem dull. Even the humble Chevy was transformed into a prize with fresh styling, startling color combinations, luxuries like power steering and air conditioning, and an all-new, powerful V-8 engine under the hood.

1955 Chevy Bel Air

By 1957, Americans were beginning to buy smaller cars in larger quantities. They snapped up sixty-four thousand Volkswagen Beetles and eighty-four thousand Ramblers that year. Detroit's auto companies responded with their own compacts. The 1960 Corvair attracted attention with its dramatic new styling and rear-mounted engine directly inspired by the Volkswagen Beetle.

1960 Corvair

Make the Connection

Other cars that feature stylists' work can be found in the Style section at the back of the Museum's *Driving America* exhibition. These include the radically styled (some say over-styled) 1958 Edsel Citation and the European-inspired 1963 Buick Riviera.

1965 Ford Mustang Convertible

THE 1965 FORD MUSTANG was an unprecedented smash, marking the beginning of a five-decade run that shows no sign of stopping. It was the right car at the right time.

Lee Iacocca, Ford Motor Company's vice president of car and truck sales in 1960, sensed an almost limitless potential in the future baby boomer market. He assembled a small team of trusted advisers to plan and develop his proposed "youth car." It had to be roomy, powerful, adaptable, relatively lightweight, and cost less than $2,500.

To save millions, the car was built on the Ford Falcon chassis. Iacocca spurred creativity by organizing a contest with in-house stylists for its design. Mustang, the name the company chose, evoked open spaces, the American West, and untamed freedom.

Did You Know?

The Mustang's rollout was masterful. Ads ran in 2,600 US newspapers, and primetime commercials appeared on all three networks the night before the launch. Some twenty-two thousand sales were tallied before the first weekend was over.

Lee Iacocca's instincts were accurate that young people wanted a car that

looked sporty, had a modest price, and could be accessorized to their individual tastes. By the end of 1965, the Mustang's first model year, almost 681,000 of these cars had been sold.

1978 Dodge Omni

THE LITTLE DODGE OMNI was a big step forward for American automakers. In October 1973, the Arab nations of OPEC (Organization of Petroleum Exporting Countries) objected to Americans' military aid to Israel during the 1973 Arab-Israeli (Yom Kippur) War and placed an embargo on oil shipped to the United States. Americans had to confront the grim reality that their passion for cars had made them too dependent on foreign oil.

Drivers were shocked when gas prices suddenly rose 80 percent. It took a few years, but American manufacturers responded with cars like this 1978 Dodge Omni. The Omni's designers were inspired by the small, fuel-efficient, front-wheel-drive Volkswagen Rabbit. It featured premium options like air conditioning while its transverse engine and front-wheel-drive layout maximized interior space. The Omni and its companion car, the Plymouth Horizon, appeared at a critical time for Chrysler, when the company sought government support to survive. Chrysler used the Omni to demonstrate that an American car company could compete with imports.

Did You Know?

During the height of the Omni's popularity, *Motor Trend* magazine chose Chrysler's Dodge Omni and its companion car, the Plymouth Horizon, as its 1978 Car of the Year, proving that small didn't have to mean basic.

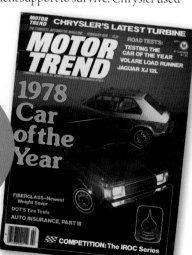

1984 Plymouth Voyager and 1991 Ford Explorer

INCREASINGLY, AMERICANS WANTED CARS THAT FIT THEIR LIFESTYLE. Just as the Mustang was introduced when baby boomers were learning to drive, the minivan came along as they were raising children and needed a roomy, economical vehicle in which to haul their family and possessions. The Chrysler minivan was truly a new kind of vehicle. It was easy to drive and could carry seven people, plus lots of luggage, camping gear, and sports equipment. Minivans were instantly popular with families and were immediately copied by both foreign and domestic manufacturers.

Sport utility vehicles—tall, boxy light trucks with high ground clearance, substantial cargo capacity, and often, four-wheel drive—had long been used by people living in rural areas. In the late 1980s, city dwellers began adopting them for ordinary driving—especially when comforts and conveniences were added. Ford's first entry into this new market, the 1991 Explorer, soon became the best-selling vehicle of its class.

1984 Plymouth Voyager, from the first model year of minivans

1991 Ford Explorer,
Ford's first SUV

Road Trips

IN THE EARLY DAYS OF MOTORING, roads were poor to nonexistent. Breakdowns and long delays frequently occurred. In 1903, this Packard became the second automobile to travel across America coast-to-coast and the first one to attempt the journey from west to east. Tom Fetch, Packard's plant foreman, and Marius C. Krarup, a journalist, made the trip from San Francisco to New York in sixty-one days.

During the late teens and 1920s, hordes of middle-class motorists answered the call of the open road. But overnight lodging was hard to find. A foldout tent trailer was the perfect solution to the lodging problem. These two-wheeled units folded down for easy car towing by day, then miraculously mushroomed into miniature homes at night.

During the depths of the Great Depression, a new form of "home on wheels" evolved from a mere curiosity to a nationwide sensation. Trailers, both home-built and factory-made, promised family togetherness in a stylish, fully equipped unit

Tom Fetch on his 1903 cross-country trip

1903 Packard Model F Runabout, nicknamed "Old Pacific"

that could be conveniently detached from the car. Wally Byam began his trailer career by publishing plans, then building trailers on a small scale. He became so impressed by the strong but lightweight Duralumin trailers of aircraft designer William Hawley Bowlus that he introduced his own Airstream version in 1936. Byam's innovative worldwide caravan tours turned the Airstream into an icon.

Gilkie tent trailer, made in Terre Haute, Indiana, about 1927

1949 Airstream Trailwind travel trailer

Make the Connection

Even the rich and famous could enjoy the freedom of the open road. Calling themselves the Vagabonds, Thomas Edison, Henry Ford, Harvey Firestone, and John Burroughs took several extended road trips together. These are recounted in the *Driving America* exhibition.

Vagabonds on old mill wheel in Lead Mine, West Virginia, 1918

Road Food

AS MOTORISTS TOOK LONGER TRIPS, an increasing variety of eateries enticed them to leave the highway and stop in for a bite to eat.

Diners were a uniquely American innovation. Motorists appreciated their convenience, reasonably priced food, and friendly atmosphere. It was easy to get started in the diner business, since diners could be purchased on an installment plan, arrived from the factory fully outfitted, and could be picked up and moved to any town or busy highway. Family members could also work for the business, keeping costs down.

After his discharge from the US Army following World War II, Clovis Lamy jumped at the opportunity to purchase and operate his own diner. He chose this model from the Worcester Lunch Car Company's catalog. The diner

LOOK CLOSER

Today, visitors can once again enjoy a bite to eat at Lamy's Diner. In outfitting his diner, Lamy balanced higher-end marble counters and mahogany trim with a less expensive stainless steel back bar and lower-cost leatherette stools and booth cushions.

had sixteen stools and four booths that held forty customers.

Meanwhile, modest food stands and more expansive drive-in restaurants also sprang up to meet motorists' needs. During the 1950s and 1960s, some of these would evolve into fast-food chains. The McDonald's franchise set the model for others. Initially, the McDonald brothers had trouble attracting capable cooks and reliable carhops to their Southern California drive-in restaurant. So they

Above: Interior of Lamy's Diner; opposite: Lamy's Diner, built by the Worcester Lunch Car Company in 1946

closed their establishment and reopened it in 1948 with a radical new Speedee Service System featuring assembly-line production of a limited menu at drastically reduced prices. Milkshake machine salesman Ray Kroc franchised the McDonald's concept in 1955.

Sign from a McDonald's in Madison Heights, Michigan, originally installed in 1960

Texaco Station

DRIVERS PURCHASED GASOLINE for their cars at grocery or hardware stores until stand-alone gas stations appeared in the 1920s. At these gas stations, oil companies and independent operators sold basically the same gasoline, so station managers found they had to compete on price and services. By the 1930s, uniformed attendants greeted drivers. Besides filling the gas tank, they checked the oil level and tire pressure. They even cleaned the windshield. Stations sold tires, batteries, and auto accessories along with cold drinks. Free road maps were often available.

Competition between service stations soon led to unique building designs to attract the attention of passing motorists. In 1937, Texaco hired visionary industrial designer Walter Dorwin Teague to redesign and modernize its stations. By 1940, Texaco boasted five hundred stations across the country sporting clean white porcelain, horizontal green lines, and bold red stars. Teague's modern design beckoned drivers, promising friendly attendants, quality gasoline, and clean restrooms.

LOOK CLOSER

The supplies stocked inside the 1940s-era Texaco station office in *Driving America* date to a time when people maintained their own cars. Younger visitors can pretend to be auto mechanics in the interactive service bay next to the office.

1931 Bugatti Type 41 Royale

THE 1931 BUGATTI TYPE 41 ROYALE, with its original selling price of $43,000, is one of the rarest automobiles in the world. It is recognized as the epitome of style and elegance in automotive design. When

built, it was longer than a Duesenberg, had twice the horsepower of a Rolls-Royce, and was more costly than both put together.

This is the third Bugatti Royale ever produced. Its chassis was built by Bugatti Automobiles S.A.S. in France and its body crafted by Ludwig Weinberger in Munich, Germany. German physician Joseph Fuchs was its original owner. In 1943, the Bugatti passed from Dr. Fuchs—by then living in New York—to Charles Chayne, chief engineer at Buick. He had it restored, made several modifications to it, and changed the paint scheme from black with yellow trim to white and green. In 1958, Chayne—by then a vice president at General Motors—donated the Bugatti to The Henry Ford so that more people could enjoy it.

Did You Know?

Not only did the Bugatti Royale do everything on a grander scale than the world's other great luxury cars, it was also more rare. Bugatti built only six Royales, whereas there were 481 Model J Duesenbergs and 1,767 Phantom II Rolls-Royces.

Early Buses

THE POPULARITY OF CITIES AS VACATION DESTINATIONS inspired manufacturers to develop special vehicles for tourists, such as the open-sided twelve-passenger vehicle made in 1906 by the Rapid Motor Vehicle Company of Pontiac, Michigan. This so-called "Rapid Bus" could shuttle travelers to and from hotels and rail depots or carry groups of tourists on sightseeing trips. Its top speed of fifteen miles per hour *was* rapid in 1906!

Also on exhibit in the Museum is the first school bus made by Blue Bird, one of the country's most significant school bus builders. In 1925, a customer stopped by Albert Luce's Fort Valley, Georgia, Ford dealership to order a bus that could transport his workers to his cement plant. But the rickety wooden body that Luce devised—traversing the area's bumpy, unpaved roads—began rattling apart before the customer could finish paying for the bus. By 1927, the determined Luce had developed a stronger steel body. He soon began making purpose-built steel-framed school buses full time.

1906 "Rapid Bus"

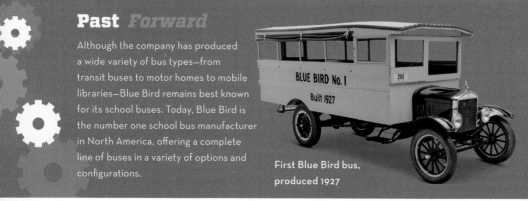

Past *Forward*

Although the company has produced a wide variety of bus types—from transit buses to motor homes to mobile libraries—Blue Bird remains best known for its school buses. Today, Blue Bird is the number one school bus manufacturer in North America, offering a complete line of buses in a variety of options and configurations.

First Blue Bird bus, produced 1927

1901 Ford "Sweepstakes" Race Car

IN THE SUMMER OF 1901, things were not going well for Henry Ford. His first car company, the Detroit Automobile Company, had failed, and his financial backers had doubts about his talents as an engineer and as a businessman. Building a successful race car, he thought, would reestablish his credibility.

Ford worked with several talented associates to design and build "Sweepstakes." He entered it in a race that took place on October 10, 1901, at a horse-racing track in Grosse Pointe, Michigan. His only opponent was Alexander Winton, an already successful auto manufacturer and the country's best-known race car driver. No one believed the inexperienced, unknown Ford had a chance to win.

When the race began, Ford fell behind immediately, trailing by as much as three hundred yards. But he quickly improved his driving technique, gradually cutting into Winton's lead. Then Winton's car developed mechanical trouble, and Ford swept past him on the main straightaway as the crowd roared its approval.

Henry Ford driving "Sweepstakes," with Ed "Spider" Huff (who worked on the electrical system) kneeling on running board, 1901

1906 Locomobile "Old 16"

THE YEAR 1908 WAS A TURNING POINT for the American automobile industry. Henry Ford introduced the Model T. William Durant incorporated General Motors. The Thomas Flyer, a car built in Buffalo, New York, won the New York-to-Paris race, beating several European rivals. And this Locomobile, driven by George Robertson, won the prestigious Vanderbilt Cup Race on Long Island, New York—the first American car to win a major international automobile race.

Millionaire automobile enthusiast William K. Vanderbilt had begun this race in 1903 to encourage improvements in the quality of American cars. But French cars won year after year. The Locomobile set the fastest lap in the 1906 Vanderbilt Cup, but repeated tire failures resulted in a tenth-place finish. In 1908, with improved tires, the thundering Locomobile swept to victory. It became affectionately known as "Old 16," its number in that famous race. Later owners—one of whom had helped build the original car, another who had seen the 1908 race—lovingly kept it in original running condition.

> ## Did You Know?
> Unlike today's race cars, "Old 16" required two people to handle it—a driver and a "mechanician." The mechanician pressurized the fuel tank with the hand pump, regulated oil flow, changed tires, and hand-cranked the massive engine if it stalled.

Bob and Bill Summers with Goldenrod, Bonneville Salt Flats, Utah, 1965

1965 Goldenrod
Land Speed Race Car

BUILDERS BOB AND BILL SUMMERS were part of an automobile culture unique to Southern California—a "hot rod economy" of people who made their living building cars and equipment, promoting races, operating tracks, selling equipment and accessories, and writing about cars and events. In 1963, they decided to pursue the wheel-driven (as opposed to jet- or rocket-powered) land speed record of 394.196 miles per hour at Utah's vast Bonneville Salt Flats. The previous record had been set in 1947 by John Cobb, one of a succession of wealthy Englishmen who drove well-financed cars powered by huge airplane engines.

In November 1965, this sleek car flashed across the Bonneville Salt Flats at 409.277 miles per hour to break the world speed record for wheel-driven cars. Keys to its success were its long, slim shape—minimizing wind resistance—and clever engineering that packed four Chrysler Hemi engines and the machinery to drive all four wheels inside that shape. Goldenrod's record would stand for over twenty-five years.

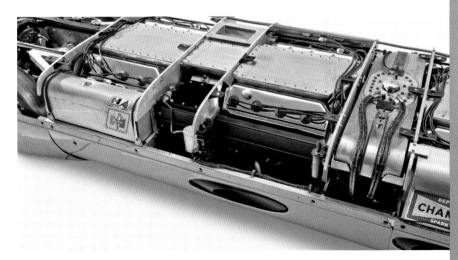

1965 Lotus-Ford Indy Race Car

THE 1965 LOTUS-FORD, the first rear-engine car to win the Indianapolis 500, is one of the seminal cars in American racing history.

From its beginning in 1911, the Indianapolis 500 has been the most prestigious automobile race in the United States. But in the early 1960s, it was falling behind the technological times. Light rear-engine cars lit up Formula One circuits everywhere, while Indy remained tied to heavy front-engine roadsters that had not fundamentally changed in a decade.

Legendary American road racer Dan Gurney concluded that the proper application of European Formula One technology could reinvigorate Indy racing. He brought Ford Motor Company together with Colin Chapman, an English designer and builder of Lotus sports and racing cars. The partnership resulted in a lightweight Lotus chassis powered by a specially designed Ford V-8 engine. The Lotus-Ford was smaller, lighter, and had much better handling than the traditional Indy cars. In 1965, Scotsman Jimmy Clark drove this car to victory in the Indianapolis 500. It established a new paradigm for American race cars.

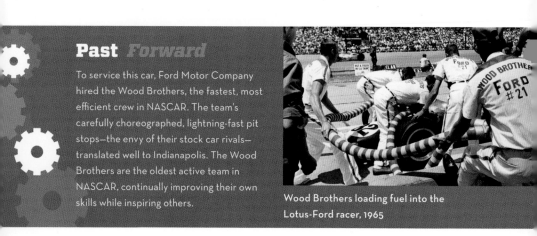

Past *Forward*

To service this car, Ford Motor Company hired the Wood Brothers, the fastest, most efficient crew in NASCAR. The team's carefully choreographed, lightning-fast pit stops—the envy of their stock car rivals— translated well to Indianapolis. The Wood Brothers are the oldest active team in NASCAR, continually improving their own skills while inspiring others.

Wood Brothers loading fuel into the Lotus-Ford racer, 1965

1967 Ford Mark IV
Sports Racing Car

THIS ALL-AMERICAN CAR WON the world's most important sports car race, the 24 Hours of Le Mans. Ford set out to beat the Europeans, particularly Ferrari. For decades, Europeans had dominated sports-car racing by using cars with small, fast-turning, highly efficient engines. But in 1967, American legends Dan Gurney and A. J. Foyt drove the Ford Mark IV to beat the second-place Ferrari by thirty-two miles at a record-breaking average speed of 135.48 miles per hour.

The car's sophisticated chassis was built of aluminum honeycomb borrowed from aerospace techniques, while the body shape was the result of hours of wind tunnel testing. Its large, rather primitive V-8 engine proved to be highly reliable when stacked up against more advanced but temperamental European designs.

During the 1960s, Ford Motor Company made a massive sports car racing effort for an American company and won Le Mans every year from 1966 to 1969. Carroll Shelby, a skilled and colorful figure in American racing history, managed the Ford team.

Did You Know?

Rather than taking a swig from the champagne bottle he received after winning the 1967 race, Dan Gurney shook it and sprayed the crowd with it. He later claimed the act was spontaneous. Planned or not, a new tradition was born.

Presidential Vehicles

THE PRESIDENT'S DESIRE to be close to the public has also made the country's chief executive difficult to protect. The many innovative features in these presidential vehicles represent the changing balance between public access and security.

President Theodore Roosevelt was not fond of automobiles and rarely used one. He preferred the old-fashioned horse-drawn carriage for public parades and outings. In this luxurious 1902 brougham (pronounced "broam"), two passengers could sit in privacy inside while a coachman out front drove the horses.

White House staff wrote up five pages of special instructions with the order for a new presidential vehicle in 1939—the first car modified expressly for presidential

President Theodore
Roosevelt's 1902 brougham

1939 "Sunshine Special" used by
President Franklin Delano Roosevelt

service. A world war was looming, and added security was crucial. Even more security features were added in 1942, after the United States entered World War II. Other features of this custom-made car made it easier to lift President Franklin D. Roosevelt in and out, since his legs were paralyzed from the incurable disease of polio. Despite these hard-ships, President Roosevelt enjoyed rid-ing in public, and the top of his "Sunshine Special" convertible was often down as he greeted crowds.

LOOK CLOSER

Several special features were designed for Secret Service agents to ride on the sides and in back of the 1939 "Sunshine Special," below left: extra-wide running boards, platforms at the rear corners, and handles at the rear and sides of the windshield.

President Truman first rode in this flashy new 1950 convertible. President Eisenhower later had the car fitted out with a removable plexiglass top that allowed him to see and be seen even in bad weather. This "bubbletop" soon became the name for the car.

1950 "Bubbletop" used by President Dwight D. Eisenhower

Interior of the "Bubbletop" limousine

Kennedy and Reagan Cars

WHEN COMPLETED IN 1961, the sleek, modern Lincoln Continental seemed perfectly suited for the young, forward-thinking president who had just taken office—John F. Kennedy. After its assembly, the limousine was customized and modified with steps and handholds for Secret Service agents, removable roof sections, a hydraulic rear seat to elevate the president, and interior floodlights to illuminate him at night. The car was also extended three-and-one-half feet in length and painted a deep metallic blue.

President Kennedy used the 1961 limousine in many parades. But tragedy struck when he was assassinated in November 1963 while

Did You Know?

Modifications to the 1961 limousine after President Kennedy's assassination included an armored steel top and body, bulletproof glass on fixed windows, a gas tank filled with a protective foam called Safom, and solid aluminum "tires" inside the pneumatic rubber tires.

Left: President Kennedy and Ethiopian Emperor Haile Selassie in original blue-painted presidential limousine, Washington, DC, 1961; right: detail of 1961 limousine with bullet-resistant glass window, added 1964

Opposite: 1961 presidential limousine used by John F. Kennedy; above: 1972 presidential limousine used by Ronald Reagan

riding in this car through the streets of Dallas, Texas. As the world mourned, the Secret Service quickly took steps to have the vehicle rebuilt to better protect future presidents. Later modifications during Lyndon Johnson's and Richard Nixon's presidencies only served to illustrate the continual tension between the presidents' desire to be seen and the Secret Service's efforts to protect them.

The 1972 Lincoln Continental provided refuge to President Ronald Reagan in 1981 after he was shot by would-be assassin John Hinckley Jr. Like all presidential vehicles after President Kennedy's assassination, this particular car was a completely armored closed car with a permanent roof and bulletproof glass. But, in a concession to the presidents' insistence on visibility, a sunroof panel could be opened for two people to stand with their upper bodies outside the car.

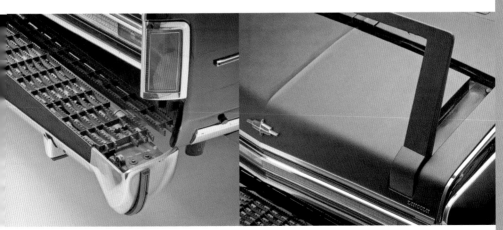

Details of footstep and handrail for Secret Service on 1972 presidential limousine

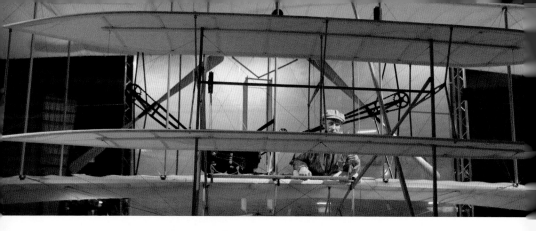

Replica 1903 Wright Flyer

DURING THE LATE 1800s, both European and American enthusiasts combined imagination with practical research to create hot-air balloons, gliders, airships, and experimental engine-driven planes to prove that people could fly. Into this universe entered Orville and Wilbur Wright. The Wright brothers brought with them an appreciation for the limits of the physical world, knowledge of work completed to date, and an extraordinary ability to imagine and collaboratively work through the possibilities available within those limits. They also brought their passion. Although their first short powered flights took place in 1903, it was not until the Wright brothers proved the superiority of their plane in France five years later that they received their first major publicity.

This full-size replica of the original 1903 Wright flyer was built by Ken Hyde and his team to commemorate the one hundredth anniversary of the Wright brothers' momentous first flights. Unfortunately, rain and low wind speed prevented this flyer from re-creating the Wrights' original flight in Kill Devil Hills, near Kitty Hawk, North Carolina, on December 17, 2003.

Make the Connection

In Greenfield Village, visitors can view the actual home where Wilbur and Orville grew up in Dayton, Ohio, as well as the bicycle shop in which they built the powered plane that provided the inspiration for the 2003 replica.

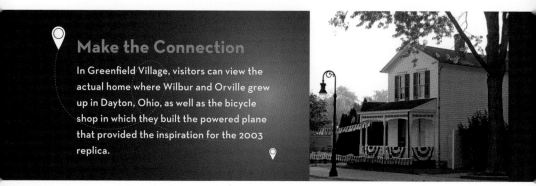

1915 Laird Biplane "Boneshaker"

TO SHOW THE PUBLIC WHAT AIRPLANES COULD DO—and simply to stay in business during the early years—manufacturers staged traveling air shows and meets. Male and some female pilots performed daring aerial feats as they barnstormed around the country. Crowds of eager spectators flocked to circuses, carnivals, and county fairs, eagerly shelling out hard-earned cash simply for the privilege of watching these wondrous acrobatics.

Matty Laird, a self-taught pilot and aircraft engineer, built this single-engine biplane when he was just twenty years old. He dubbed it the "Boneshaker" and used the plane for stunt-flying exhibitions from Montana to Maryland. This plane was one of the first to perform a loop-the-loop.

> ### Did You Know?
> Like Katherine Stinson, many other women gained fame as barnstormers—until too many tragic accidents and the resulting negative press grounded them. These included Bessie Coleman—the first licensed African American pilot in the world—and daredevil wing walker Lillian Boyer.

The Laird biplane was also flown by Katherine Stinson, an adventurous early female stunt flier. Nicknamed by the press as "The Flying Schoolgirl," Stinson was described as "a tiny woman with a big smile." During 1916 and 1917, "Kitty" Stinson flew this biplane in a barnstorming tour of the Orient. She was the first woman to fly there.

Henry Ford's Aviation Contributions

Henry Ford never liked airplanes, at least not enough to fly in them. But he appreciated their commercial potential. Intent on profiting from this new mode of transportation, he contributed substantially to the early development of commercial aviation in the United States.

The Ford Tri-Motor was the most successful airliner and cargo plane of its day. It was based on the ideas of aeronautical experimenter and promoter William Stout, who

Did You Know?

Admiral Richard Byrd achieved notoriety in 1926 by claiming that he had flown over the North Pole in a Fokker Tri-Motor. This claim was later disputed, unlike his successful 1929 flight over the South Pole in a Ford Tri-Motor.

Right: Edsel Ford, Rear Admiral Richard Byrd, and Henry Ford with 1926 Ford Tri-Motor 4-AT-1; above: Ford Tri-Motor 4-AT-B, made in 1928 by the Stout Metal Airplane Company, a division of Ford Motor Company

Radio range beacon building used at Ford airport, 1927

strongly advocated all-metal aircraft construction. The Ford Tri-Motor 4-AT-B quickly gained a reputation for ruggedness and reliability, and it was widely adopted by the growing airline companies. These features also convinced Admiral Richard Byrd to choose a Ford Tri-Motor for his attempt to be the first person to fly over the South Pole.

LOOK CLOSER

The radio range beacon house and equipment from the Ford airport can be seen in *Heroes of the Sky*, accompanied by an interactive in which visitors can try their hand at navigating like a pilot would have done.

Perhaps Ford's most important contribution to aviation, however, was his advancement in radio and navigation aids. Before this time, pilots had to depend on what they could see on the ground to get from place to place. The radio range beacon that Ford developed helped pilots stay on course through fog, rain, snow, and darkness. In 1927, it was installed in a station on the grounds of his airport. By 1933, ninety other stations had been established, aiding pilots over eighteen thousand miles of airways. The radio range beacon's value soon became so obvious that the United States government decided to operate all radio ranges, and Ford Motor Company handed over its licenses.

1920 Dayton-Wright RB-1 Monoplane

AIR RACES HELPED PROVE THE VIABILITY of aviation during its early years. The RB-1 was one of the most sophisticated aircraft to enter the 1920 Gordon Bennett race, an international air race sponsored by American newspaper publisher James Gordon Bennett. This slick new plane employed several groundbreaking innovations: a single wing rather than the usual two, wing flaps for greater control, retractable landing gear that pulled up under the fuselage after takeoff, and a monocoque fuselage—a rigid streamlined shell rather than the usual fabric covering. In addition, the enclosed cockpit replaced the usual open pilot seat. Together, these innovations allowed the craft to reach a record-breaking speed of 165 miles per hour.

The RB-1 was America's leading contender in the 1920 race. Unfortunately, a cable snapped early in the race and pilot Howard Rinehart had to pull out. Some

say that the plane incorporated too many innovations to make for a successful aircraft. It would take years, but many of this plane's advances would later be widely adopted.

Make the Connection

Heroes of the Sky includes the stories of many other aviators who broke records, like Glenn Curtiss, Jimmy Doolittle, Harriet Quimby, Wiley Post, African Americans James Banning and Thomas Allen, and larger-than-life celebrities Charles Lindbergh and Amelia Earhart.

Harriet Quimby with her Moisant monoplane, about 1911

1939 Sikorsky VS-300A Helicopter

THE HELICOPTER, A CRAFT that could hover over one spot or fly in any desired direction, was Russian immigrant Igor Sikorsky's lifelong obsession. His first attempts to build full-size helicopters in 1909 and 1910 (while still in Russia) failed because the appropriate technology did not exist yet. He subsequently spent many years (in Russia, then in the United States after immigrating in 1919) developing fixed-wing airplanes, including some of the world's most successful flying boats.

In the mid-1930s, Sikorsky returned to experimenting with helicopters. A gifted aeronautical engineer, he was empirical in his testing, sifting through previous designs to solve problems. Finally, his VS-300 made its first flight on September 14, 1939. As Sikorsky and his engineers learned more, the craft went through four major revisions and dozens of small changes. The final version flew in December 1941 and led to the development of the world's first production helicopter, the R-4, in 1942. The Museum's helicopter is the final version of the VS-300, which Sikorsky himself flew here in 1943.

Past *Forward*

From the beginning, Igor Sikorsky envisioned a range of humanitarian uses for the helicopter and that indeed became its most important legacy. The helicopter has become integral to both civilian and military aviation worldwide. Today, it is considered the premier saver of lives in accidents, disasters, and combat situations.

Igor Sikorsky landing the VS-300 helicopter on Museum grounds, 1943

1939 Douglas DC-3 Airplane

THE DC-3 WAS A WATERSHED AIRCRAFT, both financially and technologically. It was part of a new generation of trendsetting 1930s-era passenger airplanes, and it ensured aviation's permanent role in people's lives.

Introduced as a sleeper version (the DST, or Douglas Sleeper Transport) in 1935, its advantages were so clear that by 1938, 95 percent of all US commercial airline traffic occurred on DC-3s. The airplane combined a number of technical advances: cantilever wings, all-metal construction, two radial engines with cowling (removable covers), retractable landing gear, trailing edge flaps, automatic pilot, and two sets of instruments.

Did You Know?

This DC-3 flew more than twelve million miles in 83,032 hours for Eastern Airlines and North Central Airlines. When donated to The Henry Ford in 1974, it had spent more time aloft than any other airplane in history.

The Museum's DC-3 airplane as a North Central plane, 1965–74

Cockpit of 1939 Douglas DC-3 airplane

The DC-3 was the result of the visionary efforts of multitalented engineer and entrepreneur Donald Douglas. Inspired by a flying demonstration given by Orville Wright in 1909, Douglas quit his plan to join the navy and studied aeronautical engineering instead. He realized that creating a plane for passengers meant more than just building an airplane that performed well. Passengers wanted to be comfortable. The long, sleek DC-3, introduced in 1936, comfortably seated twenty-one passengers—allowing airlines for the first time to make money by carrying only passengers without the extra burden of transporting airmail.

Cyrus "C. R." Smith, head of American Airlines, called the DC-3 "the perfect airplane." It set a new standard for the industry. Douglas claimed, "One thing seems certain—the DC-3 converted millions of ground lubbers to the acceptance of air travel as a safe and practical means of transportation."

Detail from a 1954 American Airlines booklet showing the comforts of passenger travel on a DC-3

Bagley Avenue Workshop

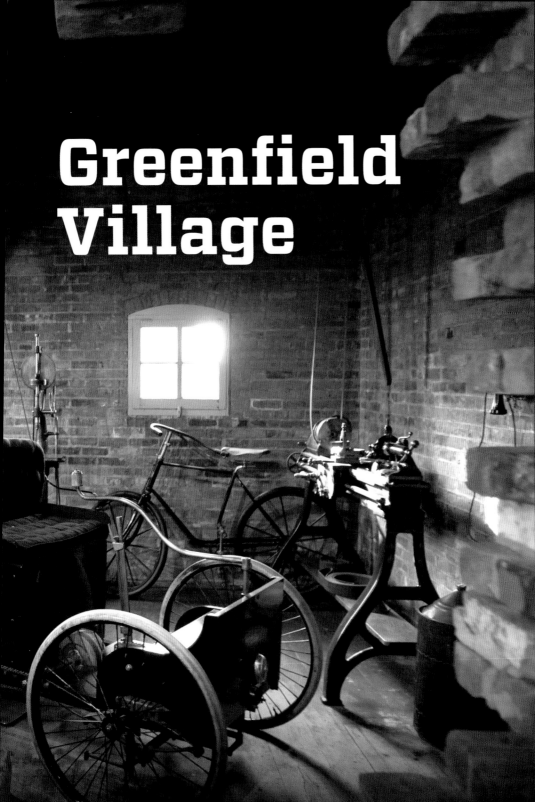

Greenfield Village

"As a nation, we have not depended so much on the rare or occasional genius as on the general resourcefulness of our people. That is our true genius, and I am hoping that Greenfield Village will serve that."

Greenfield Village

Greenfield Village is not really a village at all, though in many places it appears to be. Perhaps the best way to describe Greenfield Village is as Henry Ford's collection of buildings—representing his heroes; his personal history; and the crafts, industries, and homes that he felt both characterized the past and established a blueprint for the future.

Ford's idea of re-creating a historic village in Dearborn, Michigan, began to take shape when he restored his own birthplace (1919) and childhood school (1923) a few miles away from what is now Greenfield Village. He chose a plot of land in the midst of Ford Motor Company property and engaged Ford draftsman Edward J. Cutler to make drawings and ensure that buildings were going up according to plan. Sometimes Cutler had only a few weeks to completely dismantle a building, ship it to Dearborn, and rebuild it. Other times, the buildings were designed right in the Village at Ford's request.

A flurry of moving and construction occurred just in time for the October 21, 1929, dedication, which marked the fiftieth anniversary of Thomas Edison's invention of his workable incandescent electric lamp. Ford continued to add buildings afterward, at times relocating them to suit his thinking. By the mid-1940s, he had collected over seventy buildings—most of which still make up Greenfield Village today. Buildings added since that time include Heinz House, Daggett and Firestone Farmhouses, and the DT&M Roundhouse.

One of Henry Ford's earliest and most cherished ideas for Greenfield Village was re-creating Thomas Edison's research laboratory, opposite.

After visitors "walk through" Henry Ford's early life and influences in this area, they can ride in a real Model T.

Henry Ford's Model T

I n this district, visitors can trace the life of Henry Ford from childhood all the way to the achievement of his dream—the creation of the Model T.

The journey begins at the farmhouse where Henry Ford was born in 1863. It then highlights milestone moments from his early life that led Ford to create the Model T in 1908, the "universal car" that changed the world. Each of these milestones illuminates aspects of the character, determination, and vision that ultimately led Ford to become one of America's greatest industrialists and innovators.

Here, landscapes and settings change from the fields and farmyards around Henry Ford's birthplace, to the backyard shed behind his home on Bagley Avenue in Detroit, to the brick factory alley and courtyard adjacent to the Ford Motor Company building. The urban setting continues behind the factory building, where visitors can take their own ride in a Model T.

Henry Ford driving his Quadricycle through the streets of Detroit, October 1896

Ford Home

HENRY FORD WAS BORN AND RAISED IN THIS FARMHOUSE, originally built in 1860 or 1861 a few miles northeast of where Greenfield Village is now located. Henry was the eldest of William and Mary Ford's six children. William, a hard-working farmer, was a solid figure in the community, while Mary was passionate about her family and about keeping the house clean and in order.

Although he loved his parents, Henry hated the drudgery of farm work. He often felt that there had to be ways to make it easier. From an early age, Henry was far more interested in machines. His parents didn't discourage him. His mother, especially, nurtured this interest. It was this passion for machines that carried six-teen-year-old Henry away from the family farm and into the city of Detroit to try his hand at being a machinist.

Henry Ford, approximately three years old

In 1919, Henry Ford—by then a wealthy, successful industrialist who was thinking about preserving his own history—began restoring his childhood home on its original site. He furnished the farmhouse the way he remembered it from the time of his mother's death in 1876, when he was thirteen. Ford and his assistants combed the countryside for items.

The Ford homestead on its original site, 1930

According to his sister Margaret, "he left no stone unturned."

Ford moved the farmhouse to Greenfield Village in 1944, and it opened to the public in 1953.

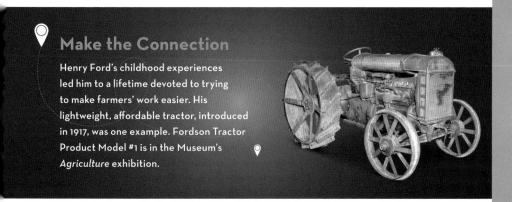

Make the Connection

Henry Ford's childhood experiences led him to a lifetime devoted to trying to make farmers' work easier. His lightweight, affordable tractor, introduced in 1917, was one example. Fordson Tractor Product Model #1 is in the Museum's *Agriculture* exhibition.

Owl Night Lunch Wagon

HENRY FORD FREQUENTED THIS LUNCH WAGON when he worked the night shift as a steam engineer at Detroit's Edison Illuminating Company (later Detroit Edison) in the 1890s. The Owl, which specialized in hot dogs, coffee, and pies, is thought to be the last surviving night lunch wagon. Horses hauled out wagons like these onto city streets after regular restaurants closed for the night. Night lunch wagons offered simple, affordable food to hungry workers on the night shift, theatergoers, policemen on the night beat, and other people who stayed out late at night. Originating in New England, lunch wagons spread across the country to cities like New York, Detroit, Chicago, and Denver.

Henry Ford purchased the Owl Night Lunch Wagon in 1927 after Detroit banned these wagons from city streets because of traffic congestion. The Owl was given a fresh coat of paint and served as the first food establishment in Greenfield Village. Completely refurbished in the 1980s, the Owl is still in operation today.

Visitors ordering food at the Owl Night Lunch Wagon, Greenfield Village, 1935

Past *Forward*

Lunch wagons have returned in the form of gourmet food trucks. Much like lunch wagon proprietors, food truck operators offer handheld specialties at modest prices. Today, special parks have been created in major cities to house food trucks, and food truck festivals and rallies draw thousands of people.

Food truck at The Henry Ford's opening of the *Roadside America* exhibition, 2015

Bagley Avenue Workshop

WHILE EMPLOYED AS A STEAM ENGINEER at Edison Illuminating Company in Detroit, Henry Ford worked in his spare time on his dream of creating a self-propelled gasoline-powered automobile. Successful experiments by others had fueled his interest in the idea. His first success came in 1893, when he created an operating gasoline engine, which he test-ran on the kitchen sink in his home with his wife Clara's help. Then, with assistance from knowledgeable and talented coworkers, Ford created a working automobile in the shed behind his and Clara's rented duplex at 58 Bagley Avenue. After more than two years of experimentation, Ford finally completed his first working automobile, the Quadricycle. On June 4, 1896, thirty-two-year-old Henry Ford proudly drove his automobile through the streets of Detroit.

Did You Know?

When Ford completed his Quadricycle in 1896, he realized that the shed door was too small for him to move his invention outside. So he used an ax to widen the door.

Ford later returned to the 58 Bagley Avenue duplex searching for this piece of his personal history. The shed had been torn down, but he obtained some bricks and two windows from the Bagley Avenue home to re-create this shed in Greenfield Village in 1933.

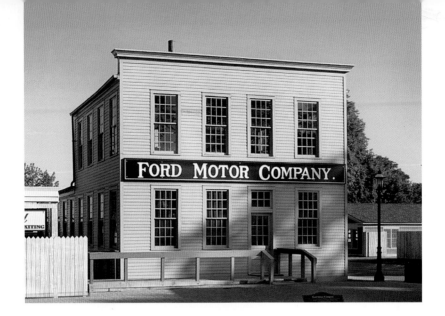

Mack Avenue Plant

BUILT IN 1945 IN GREENFIELD VILLAGE, this building is a scaled-down re-creation of Henry Ford's first Ford Motor Company factory, located on Mack Avenue in Detroit. Ironically, the original building had housed a shop that made horse-drawn wagons.

At the Mack Avenue Plant in 1903, Ford's capable young workers assembled the company's first production automobiles—Model As—from components produced by local manufacturers. Within eighteen months, the company outgrew this factory and moved to a larger facility on Piquette Avenue in Detroit, where a series of subsequent automobile models were produced.

In 1908, working with a handpicked group of employees, Henry Ford finally achieved his vision of creating a "motorcar for the great multitude"—the Model T. To supply the huge and almost immediate demand, he followed up at his next plant in Highland Park with a moving assembly line to produce these cars in ever-greater numbers. Then he stunned the world by doubling workers' wages to five dollars a day—presumably to attract enough workers to assemble them.

LOOK CLOSER

The large safe in this building comes from the actual Mack Avenue Plant. It is said to have been used by Alexander Malcomson, the company's first treasurer. The first Ford Motor Company checkbook is also in The Henry Ford's collection.

By the mid-1920s, Model Ts were everywhere. The "Tin Lizzie" was the best-selling car in the world, and Henry Ford's auto company had grown to become one of the world's biggest businesses. More than fifteen million of these cars were produced and sold between 1908 and 1927, a record that surpassed every other car until the Volkswagen Beetle.

Assembly line at Highland Park Plant, about 1925

As a boy, Henry Ford attended the one-room Scotch Settlement School, now located on the Village Green.

Main Street

In every town, Main Street was just as its name implied—the main artery of commerce through the town's business district. In a larger sense, these businesses represented the community's aspirations. They were evidence of the town's growth and prosperity, symbols of pride to show visitors. Main Streets teemed with activity. They were the places to see and be seen, to meet, talk, shop, and celebrate community events together.

The Main Street district in Greenfield Village combines two distinctive areas. In the busy commercial district—which includes the Wright Cycle Shop, Cohen Millinery, and Grimm Jewelry Store—visitors can watch parades of vehicles, dramatic performances, and live music and dancing during special events. Then, past the working carousel and the all-abilities playground stands a cluster of buildings located around Henry Ford's first and oldest idea for Greenfield Village: a village green or commons like the ones he saw on visits to New England. These buildings include Eagle Tavern, Martha-Mary Chapel, Scotch Settlement School, and Logan County Courthouse.

Eagle Tavern building on its original site in Clinton, Michigan, about 1905

Wright Home

WILBUR AND ORVILLE WRIGHT lived in this home—built in 1870 and originally located in Dayton, Ohio—while they developed their first successful powered airplane. Orville was born here in 1871, and Wilbur died here in 1912. Though the family did not live here from 1877 to 1884, the Wright brothers always thought of this building as home.

Their mother, Susan, had died before they started experimenting with airplanes, but she had always encouraged her sons to work with tools and machines. Their father, Bishop Milton Wright, encouraged the boys and their younger sister, Katharine, to be intellectually curious. Their family life in this house deeply shaped the brothers' character, values, and ability to achieve their dream.

Did You Know?

Orville and Wilbur Wright made their own home improvements, building the house's wraparound porch and fireplace mantelpiece, redesigning the interior stairway, refinishing the decorative trim, adding wallpaper, and laying new carpet.

Orville and Wilbur Wright on the porch of their family home in Dayton, Ohio, about 1910

On May 30, 1899, Wilbur wrote one of the most important letters of his life in this home. It was addressed to the Smithsonian Institution in Washington, DC, requesting published works on the subject of human flight. Excited by the prospect of exploring the challenge, the brothers were about to begin a systematic study of flight that would lead to their successful 1903 flyer—the first controlled human flying machine in the world. According to David McCullough, author of the 2015 book *The Wright Brothers*, Wilbur wrote the letter while sitting at Katharine's small slant-top desk in the front parlor—still on view in the house today.

Orville Wright offered the home to Henry Ford in 1936, with many original furnishings.

Wright Cycle Shop

THE WRIGHT CYCLE SHOP may truly be called the "birthplace of aviation." This is the original building from Dayton, Ohio, in which the first and all later Wright flyers were made. It was located a few blocks from the Wright family home.

The Wright Cycle Shop was actually the sixth and last in a series of rented

structures where Wilbur and Orville ran their bicycle business. Here, they serviced bicycles, sold new and used ones, and even manufactured a few of their own under the brand names Van Cleve and St. Clair. The income from this shop financed their aviation experiments.

Between 1900 and 1908, Wilbur and Orville built all their gliders and airplanes at the cycle shop, including experimental gliders, the first powered planes, and the airplanes in which they gave their first public flying demonstrations. Charlie Taylor, their shop

The Wright brothers' first successful flight, in Kill Devil Hills, North Carolina, December 17, 1903

A Wright-produced Van Cleve bicycle is displayed on the upper shelf inside the shop.

mechanic, often assisted them.

The brothers' experience in building and fixing bicycles helped them unlock the mysteries of human flight, as did their determination, curiosity, methodical process, and collaborative thinking. John Daniels, who witnessed their successful flight in December 1903, said: "It wasn't luck that made them fly; it was hard work and common sense; they put their whole heart and soul and all their energy into an idea and they had the faith."

In 1936, Henry Ford purchased the bicycle shop. He admired the Wrights as self-made men, like himself.

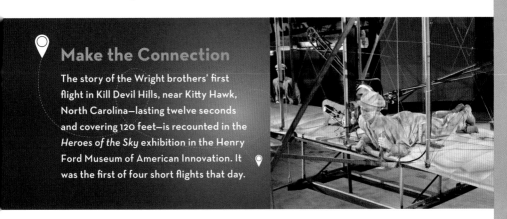

Make the Connection

The story of the Wright brothers' first flight in Kill Devil Hills, near Kitty Hawk, North Carolina—lasting twelve seconds and covering 120 feet—is recounted in the *Heroes of the Sky* exhibition in the Henry Ford Museum of American Innovation. It was the first of four short flights that day.

Grimm Jewelry Store and Cohen Millinery

THESE TWO STORES FROM DETROIT, MICHIGAN, offer a glimpse of what specialty shops were like during the late 1800s. Shops in fast-growing cities like Detroit offered a range of choices related to one type of product, as opposed to "general merchandise" stores in country villages, like the J. R. Jones General Store in Greenfield Village.

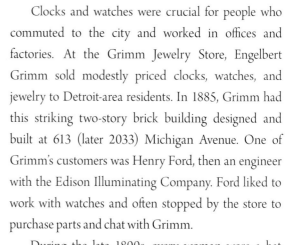

Clocks and watches were crucial for people who commuted to the city and worked in offices and factories. At the Grimm Jewelry Store, Engelbert Grimm sold modestly priced clocks, watches, and jewelry to Detroit-area residents. In 1885, Grimm had this striking two-story brick building designed and built at 613 (later 2033) Michigan Avenue. One of Grimm's customers was Henry Ford, then an engineer with the Edison Illuminating Company. Ford liked to work with watches and often stopped by the store to purchase parts and chat with Grimm.

During the late 1800s, every woman wore a hat in public, no matter her social standing. At the Cohen

Millinery shop at 444 Baker Street, Elizabeth Cohen fashioned new hats and refashioned old ones in the latest seasonal styles. Mrs. Cohen, a widow, operated the store during the 1890s. In addition to hats, she sold dry goods (fabric, thread, and sewing notions like buttons), fancy goods (ladies' fans, hair combs, and gloves), and gents' furnishings (suspenders, cravats, collars, and cuffs).

Did You Know?

Both store owners lived upstairs from their shops, a way to reduce costs and work near their families. Mrs. Cohen, a widow, could also watch over her four young children while tending to her shop.

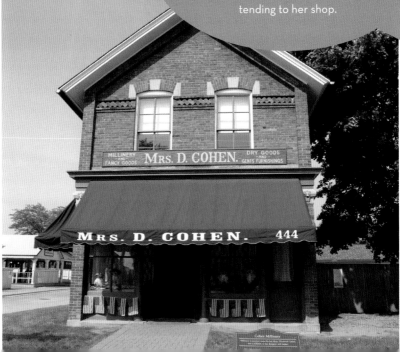

Heinz House

HENRY J. HEINZ STARTED HIS LONG AND ILLUSTRIOUS CAREER at this house, built in 1854 and originally located in Sharpsburg, Pennsylvania (about six miles east of Pittsburgh). As an enterprising youth, he peddled produce from his family's garden, finding a ready market for his bottled horseradish.

Heinz started his first company in 1869 in this house when he was just twenty-five. From horseradish, he branched out to produce celery sauce, pickled cucumbers, sauerkraut, and vinegar. His products, which emphasized quality, helped ease housewives' onerous tasks of canning and preserving. Before the days of refrigerators, his condiments and relishes added flavor to people's monotonous

diets and helped make less-than-fresh food taste more palatable.

By 1872, Heinz had moved his company to Pittsburgh. The house itself was relocated there in 1904 to become a company museum. The Heinz House was moved to Greenfield Village in 1954. Today, it features an artifact-rich exhibit focusing on the H. J. Heinz Company's innovative products, business practices, and marketing techniques.

Sir John Bennett Shop

THIS SHOP WAS ONCE A POPULAR ESTABLISHMENT on the busy commercial thoroughfare of Cheapside in London, England. Sir John Bennett was a successful third-generation clock, watch, and jewelry maker. His store occupied the building—originally five stories high—from 1846 to 1929.

Bennett hired Italian artist Brugiotti to design the mythological giants Gog and Magog to mark time by means of interior clockwork mechanisms. These figures, along with a Father Time and Muse figure, took turns striking the bells above the original store's entrance every fifteen minutes to the sound of the Westminster chimes.

Henry Ford had a lifelong interest in clocks and watches. When he learned the building was to going be demolished, he purchased and shipped the clockwork mechanism (and, later, parts of the building façade) to Dearborn. Once in Greenfield Village, Ford had his draftsman, Edward Cutler, trim the shop down to two stories to better fit the scale of the Village.

Today, the Sir John Bennett Shop houses a retail sweet shop.

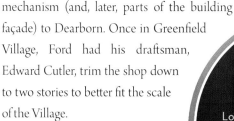

LOOK CLOSER

Look at the top of the building to spot the dragon weather vane. Its wings and tail catch the breeze, and its head—weighted with lead—balances its body, allowing it to pivot freely.

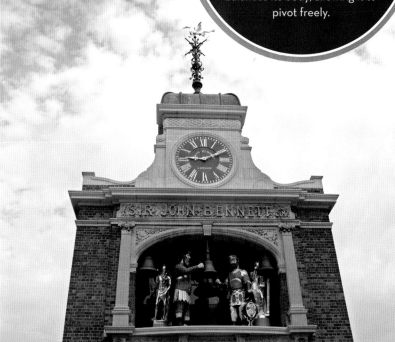

Donald F. Kosch
Village Playground

THIS ONE-OF-A-KIND PLAYGROUND is for children of all different abilities to explore, play, and learn together. It is designed to resemble a big construction site with boilers and gears, work areas, a cement mixer, and even a water tower. The playground was inspired by Virginia Lee Burton's 1939 children's classic, *Mike Mulligan and His Steam Shovel.*

The twenty-five-thousand-square-foot site is multilevel with ramps, bonded and concrete rubber surfaces that are ADA accessible, and elements constructed out of natural and authentic materials in keeping with the aesthetic of Green-

field Village. The playground opened in 2013 with a generous donation from Mary and Don Kosch. Most of the elements here were created especially for the site, but the 1931 Model AA truck and the twenty-foot-long boiler (which once sat near the Armington & Sims Machine Shop) are authentic artifacts.

The playground is geared toward children in the second grade and younger, as well as children of all ages with special needs (with adult supervision).

Herschell-Spillman Carousel

THE SUCCESS OF THE MULTIPLE AMUSEMENT PARKS at Coney Island, New York, inspired countless imitators across the country. Urban trolley lines (operating within cities) and interurban railways (operating between cities, or from cities to surrounding rural communities) helped spread the development of these parks by financing them so they could profit by transporting people to them.

The Village carousel, built around 1913 by the Herschell-Spillman Company, operated at Liberty Lake Park near Spokane, Washington. On weekends, people from Spokane rode the interurban to this park to enjoy dancing, swimming, and mechanical rides.

The Herschell-Spillman Company of North Tonawanda, New York, epitomized the innovative manufacturing techniques of American carousel builders in the early 1900s. Herschell-Spillman pro-

Did You Know?

Herschell-Spillman carousels were known for their wide variety of animals, including pigs, goats, roosters, lions, tigers, zebras, dogs, cats, storks, and giraffes. They were unique in featuring a frog, called a "hop toad" in the company's catalog.

duced affordable carousel animals through a shop production system that used carving machines to rough out the shapes and semiskilled and unskilled workers to finish the work. The company became one of the most popular and successful carousel manufacturers in the country.

This carousel was moved to Greenfield Village and restored to operating condition in 1974.

J. R. Jones General Store

THE J. R. JONES STORE was originally located in the country village of Waterford, Michigan, about thirty-five miles northwest of Detroit. James R. Jones was one of nine different proprietors who operated a general merchandise store in this building from the time it was built in 1856–57 until Henry Ford purchased it in 1927. From 1882 to 1888, Jones sold a wide array of products to townspeople and local farm families—from coffee and sugar to fabrics and trims to farm tools and hardware.

The general store in Waterford, Michigan, just before its removal to Greenfield Village, 1926

LOOK CLOSER

Look for early brand name products displayed in this store, including Heinz Pickled Cucumbers, Magic Yeast, Columbus Baking Powder, Eagle Brand Condensed Milk, Ayer's Hair Vigor, and Queen Anne Soap.

With competing stores in town, J. R. Jones did everything he could to make a go of his business. He enticed customers by selling a line of sporting goods and offering a free color print with every large bill of goods. He also stored a supply of eggs in the cellar, which he bought inexpensively from dealers and sold at a profit.

During this era of developing factory production, general stores offered an ever-increasing assortment of goods. Although Waterford was located in the country, it was connected to the great commercial center of Detroit. Regular stock and special orders were transported directly by railroad.

General stores like this served as community gathering spots where people could visit, watch the comings and goings of others, and catch the latest news. The J. R. Jones General Store also functioned as the local post office and, for a time, it had the only telephone in town.

Eagle Tavern

EAGLE TAVERN offers a historic dining experience for Village visitors, featuring food and drink re-created from mid-1800s recipes. This tavern, built in 1831–32, was originally located in Clinton, Michigan, about fifty miles southwest of Detroit. Taverns like this offered travelers a place to eat, drink, and sleep, and townspeople a spot to socialize and catch up on the latest news.

Calvin Wood ran Eagle Tavern from 1849 to 1854. Wood was also a farmer and likely supplied much of the food for his guests from his farm. Calvin's wife, Harriet, was indispensable at the tavern—cooking, preparing food, serving guests, and housekeeping. Harriet's two daughters (from a previous marriage) probably helped out, along with additional hired help from town or the neighboring countryside.

People of all types and classes mixed together in taverns. Tavern patrons ate at the same tables, slept in common

Did You Know?

Visitors to Eagle Tavern might find that their beverage comes with a hollow tube of macaroni. When curators researched the historic beverages here, they found that sticks of macaroni were perfectly appropriate to use as drink straws or "suckers."

bedrooms, and socialized in public rooms. Sometimes, as in Eagle Tavern, a tavern was large enough to have a separate ladies' parlor, leaving the barroom for the men to drink, smoke, and debate burning issues of the day.

This tavern had many different names throughout its long history, including Eagle Tavern. When Henry Ford bought the dilapidated building in 1927, he gave it the generic name Clinton Inn.

Martha-Mary Chapel and Town Hall

FROM THE BEGINNING, HENRY FORD had in mind two key buildings that should flank the ends of his village green: a church and a building for town meetings. When Ford could not acquire the specific buildings he had in mind, he had Martha-Mary Chapel and Town Hall designed and built on-site in 1929.

The design for Martha-Mary Chapel was based on a much larger Congregationalist church in Bradford, Massachusetts. Ford named it after his mother, Mary Litogot Ford, and his mother-in-law, Martha Bench Bryant. It was one of six nondenominational chapels that Ford erected and the only one built of brick. Martha-Mary Chapel has been used for weddings since 1935.

In town halls, local citizens came together for town meetings, political elections, theatrical performances, and social events. Town Hall in Greenfield Village is inspired by New England public meeting halls of the early 1800s. Representative of the spirit of participative democracy, it hosts a variety of theatrical programs and special exhibitions.

LOOK CLOSER

The bell in the tower of the chapel, likely cast during the 1820s, is attributed to Joseph Revere & Associates of Boston, Massachusetts—a foundry Joseph inherited from his more famous father, Paul Revere.

Scotch Settlement School

THE MORNING BELL SUMMONED MILLIONS OF CHILDREN from America's rural areas and villages each day to one-room schools like this one. Most children

Scotch Settlement School on its original site in Dearborn Township, Michigan, 1896

who attended these schools acquired a basic knowledge of geography, writing, reading, mathematics, and history.

Scotch Settlement School was originally built in 1861, located in what was once called the Scotch Settlement in Dearborn Township. Henry Ford attended this one-room schoolhouse from about age seven to ten. The school was one of Ford's first restoration proj-

ects. Ford restored the building in 1923 and operated it on its original site as an

experimental preschool. In September 1929, it served as the first classroom for the Edison Institute school system that Henry Ford started in the Village. At the October 1929 dedication of Greenfield Village, Ford sat at a desk in Scotch Settlement School that was situated in the same location where he had once sat. He then carved his initials into the replica desk, just as he had done on the original so many years ago.

Past Forward

The Edison Institute school system closed in 1969. Today, students attend classes in the Museum and Village as part of Henry Ford Academy, a charter high school formed in 1997 in collaboration with Ford Motor Company. In 2005, students enjoyed a visit from Microsoft founder Bill Gates, shown at right.

Left to right: Bill Gates; Bill Ford Jr.; Steve Hamp, then-president of The Henry Ford

Logan County Courthouse

WHILE HIS PRIMARY LAW PRACTICE was in the state capital of Springfield, Illinois, Abraham Lincoln also traveled to outlying courthouses to try cases—including this Postville, Illinois, courthouse, built in 1840. It was one of several stops on the 8th Judicial Circuit. Most cases were civil rather than criminal, often involving matters of land ownership.

Lincoln thrived on the judicial circuit, handling all kinds of cases and representing different types of people. He developed an extraordinary ability to listen, understand, and represent opposing viewpoints and became highly respected and trusted by clients, lawyers, and judges. Along with regular towns-people, he befriended newspaper editors and local politicians when he arrived in town. All of these experiences helped prepare him for his future role as America's sixteenth president.

To Henry Ford, Abraham Lincoln embodied the ideals of the self-made man. Ford searched for a building to memorialize Lincoln's accomplishments. When he learned of this neglected courthouse, Ford had it dismantled and reconstructed in Greenfield Village in time for the October 1929 dedication.

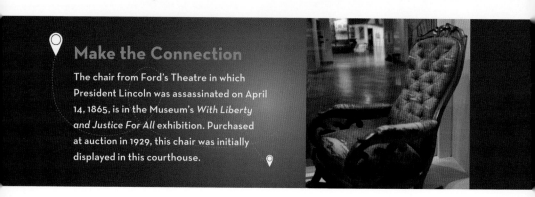

Make the Connection

The chair from Ford's Theatre in which President Lincoln was assassinated on April 14, 1865, is in the Museum's *With Liberty and Justice For All* exhibition. Purchased at auction in 1929, this chair was initially displayed in this courthouse.

Dr. Howard's Office

DR. ALONSON B. HOWARD was a country doctor who practiced medicine in rural southern Michigan from 1852 to 1883. He combined prevailing medical knowledge with his own home remedies to treat sick patients. At the time, people didn't understand that germs and unsanitary conditions caused illness and were anxious to try nearly anything to cure what ailed them. Dr. Howard would have attended to everything from pregnancies to toothaches to chronic diseases such as kidney disease and tuberculosis. He generally treated patients at his office, but he also made house calls, traveling by horse or train.

This building was constructed in 1839 as a one-room schoolhouse. It was located in Tekonsha, Michigan (about ten miles south of Marshall), in the front yard of the Howard family farm. When the school moved to a new building, Howard took it over as his office. After he died in 1883, it remained virtually intact until it moved to Greenfield Village around 1960. The doctor's office opened to the public in 1963.

LOOK CLOSER

The garden next to the office contains plants and herbs that Dr. Howard might have used in his practice to treat sick patients. Visitors can pick up a handout listing these plants and herbs inside the doctor's office.

Left: Wooden kegs with herbal remedies and root extracts; right: garden with medicinal plants and herbs behind the doctor's office

Thomas Edison operated the vacuum pump (left) with this replica lightbulb to reenact his original lighting experiment during the 1929 Light's Golden Jubilee dedication.

Edison at Work

In this district, visitors can visit the actual workspaces where Thomas Edison and his assistants developed an electric lighting system that would transform the world. The district includes Thomas Edison's Menlo Park Laboratory Complex; the Sarah Jordan Boarding House, where Edison's unmarried male workers lived; and Edison's Fort Myers Laboratory, where Edison later undertook scientific work near his winter home in Florida.

Thomas Edison was Henry Ford's biggest hero. Ford was convinced that Edison could inspire others as well, so he took on the herculean task of re-creating Edison's extensive Menlo Park, New Jersey, complex. Some buildings were moved from the original site, intact; others were reconstructed from salvaged parts or re-created on-site. Seven railcars of New Jersey clay were hauled in and spread over the compound to add authenticity. Edison himself donated hundreds of historical artifacts. At the dedication of Greenfield Village in 1929, Edison sat in a wooden chair in the Menlo Park Laboratory and reenacted the final moments of his first successful lighting experiment from fifty years earlier.

Thomas Edison (center, wearing skullcap and neckerchief) and his workers in Menlo Park Laboratory, New Jersey, 1880

Thomas Edison's Menlo Park Complex

MENLO PARK LABORATORY was Thomas Edison's "invention factory." Working intensively here from 1876 to 1882, Edison and his skilled assistants created a multitude of new marvels—including the phonograph and the first practical electric lighting system—as well as significant improvements to the telephone, the telegraph, and the electric railway. Perhaps Edison's most important invention, however, was the laboratory itself. As the world's first industrial research and development lab, it provided a model for subsequent industrial research facilities.

Edison's ability to orchestrate the invention process set him apart from other inventors. He gathered men with particular skills, scientific equipment, and raw materials; obtained financial backing; and brought an understanding of the marketplace. Equally important, Edison grasped the critical role that technology could play in business strategies and how the invention process could be organized systemically.

The original Menlo Park Laboratory was built in 1876 as a simple two-story frame structure. In 1878, Edison constructed a series of additional buildings to better accommodate his largest and most complex project yet, the electric

lighting system. The main laboratory building—particularly the second floor—remained the center of his experimental activities. An enlarged machine shop and expanded office/library also became important parts of the operation. The glass house, carpenters' shop, and carbon shed contained essential processes and skilled workers that supported the activities of the research lab.

Make the Connection

In the Museum, visitors can see Thomas Edison's distinctive signature in the cornerstone created to commemorate the founding of the Museum and Village, as well as what is alleged to be Edison's last breath inside a test tube.

137

Sarah Jordan Boarding House

MORE THAN A DOZEN UNMARRIED MALE WORKERS from Thomas Edison's Menlo Park Laboratory lived in this boarding house, returning here to eat, sleep, and spend the evening if they were not working late at the lab, as they often did. Boarders' rates varied from five to eight dollars per week, depending on the type of room and number of meals.

Sarah Jordan, a widowed distant relative of Thomas Edison's first wife, Mary, ran the boarding house with help from her adopted daughter, Ida, and a live-in maid. Running a boarding house was one of the few acceptable ways for widows like Sarah Jordan to make a living. The three women occupied one side of the first floor, while the public rooms on the other side and the upstairs bedrooms were devoted to the boarders.

Did You Know?

The Sarah Jordan Boarding House was just a short walk from Thomas Edison's laboratory complex in Menlo Park—the same distance from the complex that it is today in Greenfield Village.

Built as a duplex in 1870, the boarding house was one of three private residences to be wired for Edison's new electrical lighting system in December 1879—and is the only one still in existence.

Thomas Edison's Fort Myers Laboratory

THOMAS EDISON NEVER STOPPED WORKING, even when he spent time at his winter home in Fort Myers, Florida. He used this lab/workshop, built 1885–86, to continue experimenting with projects he was working on at his West

Orange, New Jersey, laboratory. These included electrical lighting, telegraphy, and underwater communication. In 1927, Thomas Edison, Henry Ford, and tire magnate Harvey Firestone financed and formed the Edison Botanic Research Corporation so that Edison could research natural sources of rubber. Here at this lab, and in the Botanical Laboratory built after this structure was removed to Greenfield Village, Edison tested more than seventeen thousand plants from all over

Fort Myers Laboratory on its original site, 1912. Thomas Edison is at left.

the world. He determined that the common weed goldenrod had the greatest potential for yielding rubber.

Fort Myers Laboratory was the first building to be reconstructed in Greenfield Village, in September 1928. It had a second experimental life, offering seclusion to a select group of Ford Motor Company engineers tasked with developing the Ford V-8 engine in the early 1930s.

Past *Forward*

Edison's rubber experiments came in handy when the United States and its allies needed an emergency source of rubber during World War II. But as synthetic rubber became common, the project was quickly discontinued. Today, 70 percent of the rubber used in manufacturing processes is synthetic, descended from the synthetic rubber produced at that time.

Edison with goldenrod plants used in his rubber experiments, 1926

Scholar Noah Webster completed the first truly American dictionary in this home.

Porches and Parlors

In the Porches and Parlors district, visitors can observe the lifestyles and traditions of many different people who lived in these homes, as well as various structures—like a covered bridge and windmill—that might have dotted the landscape.

Each site is intended to be experienced in its own context, immersing visitors in a time and place, from the 1760s-era rural farmhouse of Samuel Daggett's family to the stately 1820s house of dictionary writer Noah Webster; from the primitive log birthplace of schoolbook author William Holmes McGuffey to the rural Georgia home of the resourceful Mattox family. Some of the residents of these homes accomplished extraordinary things, while others were ordinary people just trying to get by from day to day. All the furnishings, landscapes, and building styles further the stories of the people who lived here. As the district name implies, social interaction was important to the people who lived in these places, whether it was with family, neighbors, or within the larger sphere of community.

Luther Burbank and Henry Ford in Burbank's experimental garden, Santa Rosa, California, 1915

Ackley Covered Bridge

BRIDGES BROUGHT LOCAL communities together by spanning difficult-to-navigate rivers and creeks. This covered bridge was built in 1832, linking farmers and villagers living on either side of a branch of Wheeling Creek in southwestern Pennsylvania. The oak timbers came from the farms of Daniel Clouse and Joshua Ackley, and the bridge was built on land owned by the Ackley family. Although a builder in the local area probably supervised the design and construction of the bridge, it is believed that many men from the community contributed their time and labor to help build it.

During the late 1800s, iron bridges replaced many of the earlier covered bridges. Henry Ford acquired this bridge in 1937, when it was scheduled to be torn down. The massive trusses (the support beams along the sides) of the aging structure were gently dismantled, then carefully trucked three hundred miles to Dearborn and reassembled on its present site.

Did You Know?

The wooden roof on a covered bridge protected the wooden trusses. When exposed to sun, wind, and rain, their life expectancy was only about ten years, but when they were covered, their life span increased tenfold.

Ackley Covered Bridge on its original site in southwestern Pennsylvania, 1936

Susquehanna Plantation

SUSQUEHANNA PLANTATION—originally covering some seven hundred acres—was one of the largest, most productive farms in southern Maryland during the 1800s. This house, probably constructed before 1820, was a common form in the geographic region of Tidewater, Maryland. It was one room deep with porches that invited cooling breezes. Today, the house appears as it would have just before the Civil War.

Susquehanna Plantation was home to the wealthy Carroll family. Like other plantation owners, Henry J. Carroll managed a self-sufficient agricultural business for profit. As such, he depended upon a system of slave labor for his and his family's economic well-being and social status.

The sixty-five enslaved African Americans who lived and worked on this plantation labored from sunup to sundown. Divided into groups and supervised by an overseer, or "driver" (enslaved work leader), they cultivated tobacco and wheat under the oppressive "gang system." They struggled to provide for themselves and their families while striving to keep their families, communities, and culture intact.

Make the Connection

While the gang system of slavery was practiced at Susquehanna Plantation, the task system was used at Hermitage Plantation, originally located in coastal Georgia. Two slave quarters from Hermitage are preserved in Greenfield Village.

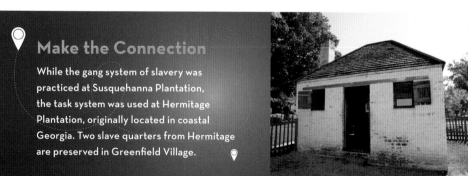

Farris Windmill

FARRIS WINDMILL is thought to be the oldest surviving windmill in the United States. It was built in the mid-1600s on the north side of Cape Cod, Massachusetts, near either the village of Sandwich or Barnstable. Later, it was moved to two different locations on the south side of Cape Cod, ending up in West Yarmouth.

Windmills like these harnessed the power of the wind in areas where strong ocean breezes and unobstructed open space provided the necessary wind force to turn the heavy wooden arms. When propelled by the wind, the arms or spars turned the three-and-one-half-ton millstones on the second floor. The ladder-like arms were originally covered with strips of canvas to help them turn.

The Farris family owned this windmill for three generations starting in 1782. When it was rebuilt in Greenfield Village in 1936, Farris Windmill was elevated on a stone foundation to provide greater public safety and to raise its arms higher into the wind.

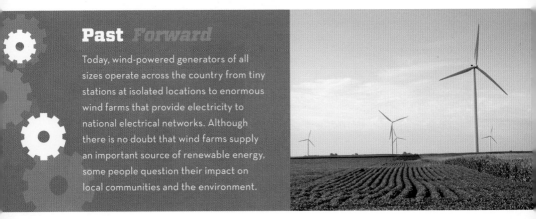

Past Forward

Today, wind-powered generators of all sizes operate across the country from tiny stations at isolated locations to enormous wind farms that provide electricity to national electrical networks. Although there is no doubt that wind farms supply an important source of renewable energy, some people question their impact on local communities and the environment.

Cotswold Cottage

PICTURESQUE COTSWOLD COTTAGE beckons visitors from the far end of Greenfield Village. Built in the early 1600s, this limestone cottage was originally located in Chedworth, Gloucestershire, in the beautiful rolling countryside of the Cotswold region of southwestern England.

This home began as a single cottage, with a second cottage added later. Throughout its life, this home changed hands several times. In the mid-1800s, it was occupied by a family of stonemasons. By the early 1900s, wealthy business-people, primarily from London, were purchasing homes like this to escape the pressures of their fast-paced lives. They added romanticized cottage gardens and furnished the interiors with comfortable, homey furniture.

Such was the case with this cottage—called Rose Cottage in the 1920s—when Henry Ford found it. Ford felt it showed how Americans' ancestors lived before they came to the United States. Even though most Americans did not actually come from the Cotswold region, people both from Henry Ford's day and today find this cottage to be a quaint reminder of the past.

LOOK CLOSER

The stable/barn was part of the original Cotswold Cottage site, while the blacksmiths' forge came from nearby. The circular dovecote, modeled after one in England, was built in Greenfield Village.

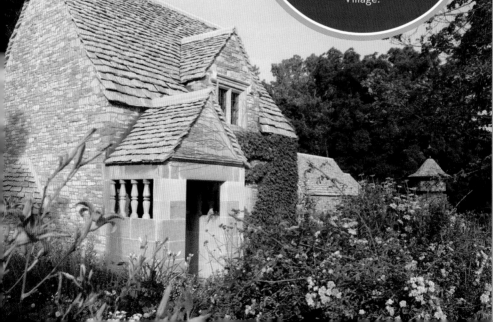

Daggett Farmhouse

AT THE DAGGETT FARMHOUSE, presenters in period clothing re-create the 1760s-era activities of the Daggett family on their Connecticut farm. Like other farm families living in hardscrabble northeastern Connecticut at the time, Samuel Daggett and his family relied largely on their own skills and hard work. Also like others, Daggett grew a diverse range of crops—wheat, rye, corn, barley, oats, hops, and tobacco—and raised a variety of livestock that included hogs, sheep, and dairy and beef cattle. Daggett's pair of oxen did the heavy work.

Did You Know?

The multipurpose hall traces its origins to rural England, where many early New England settlers came from. This room recalls the great halls of late medieval England, where much of daily life was centered.

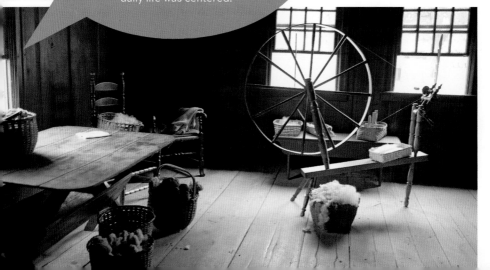

Daggett was a house builder by trade. He supplemented his family's income by hewing timber and making and mending carts, ox yokes, spinning wheels, sleds, furniture, and coffins. He even pulled teeth to earn extra income. Anna Daggett, Samuel's wife, served an equally important role on the farm. She cooked, cleaned the house, made candles, fed the barnyard animals, tended the garden and orchard, and cared for and taught their three children, Asenath, Tabitha, and Isaiah.

Like their neighbors, the Daggetts sold or traded products they made for goods and services they needed. They also relied on members of their local community for friendship and support.

Samuel Daggett built this house in Coventry (now Andover), Connecticut, in 1754, shortly after he married Anna. It was reerected in Greenfield Village in 1977.

Make the Connection

Visitors can compare the differences between how families lived in the 1760s Daggett Farmhouse (shown here) and the 1880s Firestone Farmhouse: open fireplace versus cookstove cooking, candle versus kerosene lighting, and raised-bed gardens versus the ordered rows of the Victorian kitchen garden.

Noah Webster Home

IN THIS HOUSE, SCHOLAR NOAH WEBSTER completed the first truly American dictionary: the *American Dictionary of the English Language*, published in 1828.

During his years as a student and then teacher, Webster found that children of all ages were crammed into one-room schoolhouses with no desks, few books, and untrained teachers. He wrote a textbook nicknamed the "Blue-Backed Speller" in 1783, which went on to sell more than one hundred million copies.

Did You Know?

To prepare himself for studying the origins of words and the ways in which their meanings changed throughout history, Webster learned twenty different alphabets and languages—including Greek, Latin, Hebrew, Anglo-Saxon, Welsh, Old Irish, Arabic, and Persian.

In the early 1800s, Webster began working on the seventy-thousand-entry dictionary that he would complete in this house. His dictionary aimed to capture distinctively American words and spellings for the first time.

This home was built from 1822 to 1823 in New Haven, Connecticut, for Webster and his wife, Rebecca. Intended as his retirement home, Webster worked on many publications here.

Henry Ford acquired the house in 1936, upon the recommendation of his son, Edsel, who learned of its impending demolition. Used by Edison Institute schoolchildren for many years, the Noah Webster Home was opened to the public in 1962.

Burbank Garden Office

LUTHER BURBANK, an American plant breeder and naturalist, was noted for his experiments with plants, fruits, and vegetables. In 1906, he had this office constructed on a corner of his forty-acre experimental garden in Santa Rosa, California. Burbank spent much of his time here, managing his nursery business, keeping accounts, researching, and writing.

Born on a farm in Lancaster, Massachusetts, in 1849, Burbank enjoyed experimenting with different seedlings in his mother's garden. He found one potato seedling to be so prolific that he cultivated it and successfully marketed it. Later called the Russet Burbank potato, it would become an American staple.

When Burbank was just twenty-six years old, he sold the rights to his potato variety and moved to Santa Rosa, California. For more than fifty years, Burbank conducted plant-breeding experiments here, introducing more than eight hundred new varieties of plants.

Henry Ford was inspired by Burbank's character, accomplishments, and hands-on approach. When Burbank died in 1926, his widow donated his office to Henry Ford for Greenfield Village.

Past *Forward*

The Russet Burbank potato is ideal for making crispy french fries. This potato can be cut into long thin slices, keeps a consistent texture and taste, and fries up lighter and fluffier than other varieties. French fries account for about 35 percent of the total United States utilization of potatoes.

Sounds of America Gallery

THIS HOUSE WAS BUILT AROUND 1830 in Lawrenceville (now part of Pittsburgh), Pennsylvania, where composer Stephen Collins Foster was born. When the building was brought to Greenfield Village in 1934, it was mistakenly thought to be Foster's birthplace. It is now home to an exhibit called *Sounds of America*, which explores the growth of American music through the interplay of people, musical instruments, and music itself. Topics such as music in the home, community bands, and American popular songs are covered.

Stephen Foster was one of the earliest and greatest American popular songwriters. He wrote hundreds of memorable melodies, integrating British and African American musical traditions to create a uniquely American style. Today, it's difficult

 to imagine that iconic favorites such as "Oh! Susanna," "Camptown Races," "My Old Kentucky Home," and "Beautiful Dreamer" came from the mind and pen of a single talented composer. Foster virtually invented popular music as we recognize it today, yet he died forgotten and nearly penniless at age thirty-seven.

Hermitage Slave Quarters

THESE BRICK STRUCTURES ARE JUST TWO OF THE FIFTY-TWO quarters that originally housed 201 enslaved African Americans at Hermitage Plantation in 1850.

The plantation was located on the Savannah River in coastal Georgia, just north of the city of Savannah. Henry McAlpin, a Scotsman, owned Hermitage Plantation, which totaled nearly four hundred acres in 1850. The enslaved workers here cultivated rice and manufactured bricks, rice barrels, cast-iron products, and lumber in a series of steam-powered mills.

Enslaved African Americans here worked under the "task system." Each task was carefully calculated to take eight to ten hours, and the assigned work was usually unpleasant and exhausting. Occasionally, when tasks were completed in less than a day and enslaved workers weren't helping weaker or slower workers, they could tend their own gardens, work their own crops, or produce goods for themselves or for sale.

Did You Know?

The Hermitage Slave Quarters are among the few surviving slave quarters in the United States. Southern climates, with high heat and humidity and numerous wood-eating pests, were harsh on wooden structures, especially those that were not consistently maintained.

Today, one slave quarter is furnished while the other one includes recorded accounts that reveal the endurance and courage shown by enslaved people.

Above: Former slave quarters at Hermitage Plantation in Georgia, about 1900

Mattox Family Home

THIS FARMHOUSE FROM RURAL BRYAN COUNTY, near Savannah, Georgia, was home to several generations of the Mattox family, an African American family whose determination and hard work made it possible for them to build this home in 1879 on land they had purchased.

The furnished installation at the Mattox Family Home focuses on the 1930s, when Amos and Grace Mattox—descended from enslaved African Americans—raised their children. Amos farmed, cut hair, made shoes, and preached at the local church, while Grace sewed, canned, and cooked. Today the house is furnished just as members of the Mattox family remember it.

The Mattox family belonged to a tightly knit community who shared the values of self-sufficiency, resourcefulness, and devotion to family. People were close to their neighbors—both geographically and spiritually, as they all attended services at the same church.

Today, visitors might hear 1930s-era regional music on the front porch or encounter the sights and smells of food being prepared in the kitchen.

LOOK CLOSER

The Mattox family, like families living in similar homes during this era, lined the walls of their home with newspapers not only to insulate against cool nights and winters but also to provide variety and decoration.

William Holmes McGuffey Birthplace

WILLIAM HOLMES McGUFFEY'S BIRTHPLACE was typical of many log structures that Scots-Irish families built in the densely forested area of south-western Pennsylvania in the late 1700s. Anna and Alexander McGuffey lived in this cabin after they married, and over the next five years, they had three children here. William was born in 1800. When he was two years old, the family packed up their belongings and headed farther west, seeking new opportunities in the Ohio wilderness.

As McGuffey later tried to teach in the scattered and isolated settlements of the western frontier, he saw how desperately children needed an easy, standardized method of learning to read and write. Beginning with his *First Eclectic Reader* and *Second Eclectic Readers* in 1836, McGuffey made his readers enjoyable, interesting, and accessible to children while also instilling values like virtue, industry, and thrift.

McGuffey's *Eclectic Readers* had a lasting influence on Henry Ford, who read them as a schoolboy. To honor McGuffey, Ford moved and reconstructed the educator's log birthplace in Greenfield Village in 1934.

Charles Steinmetz Cabin

CHARLES PROTEUS STEINMETZ was one of the greatest minds in the electrical world. In his day, he was likely as famous as Thomas Edison.

Standing at little more than four feet tall, Steinmetz overcame a painful spinal deformity to study mathematics and engineering at a German university. He later came to the United States and found work with General Electric Company. There, and at this cabin retreat, he devised ways to make alternating current practical and useful. Steinmetz's greatest achievements came through his application of higher mathematics to electrical problems. His calculations made long-distance electrical transmission economical, accelerating the spread of electricity into more Americans' homes.

Did You Know?

Through his innovative and prolific work at the General Electric Company from the early 1890s until his death in 1923, Charles Steinmetz virtually defined the newly emerging field of electrical engineering.

Steinmetz built this cabin—which he fondly named Camp Mohawk—as a retreat in 1896, a few years after going to work for General Electric in Schenectady, New York.

When Steinmetz's adopted son offered this cabin to Henry Ford in 1930, Ford saw its value in extending the story of electrical experimentation and innovation that he had begun with Edison's Menlo Park Complex.

Left: Interior of cabin; right: Steinmetz cabin on its original site near Schenectady, New York, 1930

George Washington Carver Cabin

GEORGE WASHINGTON CARVER was born into slavery, but he later became famous for his achievements as an agricultural chemist. He looked for ways that southern farmers could move from cotton-only farms to those that would grow a variety of crops.

George Washington Carver, 1942

For almost fifty years after receiving his college degree, Carver conducted agricultural research at Tuskegee Institute in Alabama in addition to teaching, lecturing, and writing. He performed experiments with sugar beets, cow (black-eyed) peas, and sweet potatoes. All these crops restored nitrogen to the soil and provided food for both farmers and their livestock. Carver also experimented with hybrids of cotton and with soybeans. But he is probably best known for his work with the peanut—both as an alternate crop for southern farms and as a raw material for industrial products.

Like Carver, Henry Ford shared an interest in using agricultural crops for commercial and industrial purposes. Ford had this cabin erected as a tribute to Carver in 1942.

LOOK CLOSER

The building's exterior is based on Carver's childhood memories of the Missouri slave cabin where he was born. Inside, the walls are paneled with wood from every state in the Union, symbolizing Carver's national contribution to the field of agriculture.

The Torch Lake locomotive is used to transport visitors around Greenfield Village. Like other Village locomotives, it is maintained at the DT&M Roundhouse, shown here.

Railroad Junction

Before automobiles and trucks carried people and goods across the country, railroads were the dominant form of transportation. Their networks stretched nationwide, linking towns and villages to the outside world.

Depots brought excitement and the quickened pace of urban life to small towns. The depot was also part of a system of buildings that served the railroad. Supporting structures might include grain elevators, signaling towers, produce warehouses, toolsheds, and railroad repair shops like the DT&M Roundhouse in Greenfield Village.

At Railroad Junction, visitors can board a steam-powered railroad, visit the small-town Smiths Creek Depot, and investigate the gritty work of railroad mechanics as they repair and maintain the Village's locomotives. This might include, at any given time, one of the three operating locomotives on the Weiser Railroad, the diesel-electric used as a standby, or the gasoline-mechanical used as a switching locomotive. In addition, the 1914 Baldwin 0-6-0 locomotive sits near the roundhouse, awaiting restoration, while the 1902 4-4-2 Atlantic locomotive can be viewed up close as part of the roundhouse walk-through.

Workers at the original DT&M Roundhouse, Marshall, Michigan, probably 1890s

Smiths Creek Depot

THE RAILROAD DEPOT was an important center of small town life. More than just a place to catch a train, it was here that townspeople sent and received packages and telegrams, awaited travelers, and caught up on the latest news.

Smiths Creek Depot, built in 1858, was situated on the Grand Trunk Western Railway about ten miles southwest of the thriving port city of Port Huron, Michigan. Young Thomas Edison took a job with the railway as a newsboy. He also sold candy and fresh produce on the train and at depots along the route, and he put other boys to work, claiming a share of the profits. Edison tried his hand at other things while working for the railway—telegraphy, printing, and experimenting with chemicals. Unfortunately, his work on the railway ended when his chemical experiments set a baggage car on fire alongside Smiths Creek Depot. But all these experiences contributed to the enterprising, curious, and entrepreneurial man that Edison would become.

Past *Forward*

During the late 1800s, more than forty thousand depots dotted the landscape across the United States. Today, less than half of these remain. In recent years, some local communities have preserved and adaptively reused these historically significant buildings in creative ways: as homes, hotels, museums, restaurants, visitor centers, libraries, and shopping complexes.

Union Station, Washington, D. C.

The station in this 1913 postcard is now a mixed-use intermodal transportation and shopping center.

Detroit, Toledo & Milwaukee Roundhouse

AT THE MASSIVE DT&M ROUNDHOUSE, visitors can see the Village's operating fleet of locomotives being maintained. Engineers, firemen, and mechanics carry out daily inspections, provide needed repairs, and take care of ongoing maintenance—all in full view of visitors.

While some roundhouses were literally circular buildings surrounding a turntable, the term came to be applied to any railroad maintenance facility served by a turntable. The Detroit, Toledo & Milwaukee Railroad constructed a roundhouse in Marshall, Michigan, in 1884. It continued operations through the early 1930s, when the railroad abandoned the roundhouse and its associated rail yard and shop tracks were torn up.

The DT&M facility in Marshall had badly deteriorated by the 1990s, when staff from The Henry Ford saw its potential and salvaged its extant parts to incorporate into a new, re-created roundhouse in Greenfield Village. This operating roundhouse opened in 2000.

LOOK CLOSER

The railroad turntable in front of the roundhouse was built in 1901 and originally used in Petoskey, Michigan, by the Pere Marquette Railroad. It was designed so that heavy locomotives could be moved with a minimum of workers.

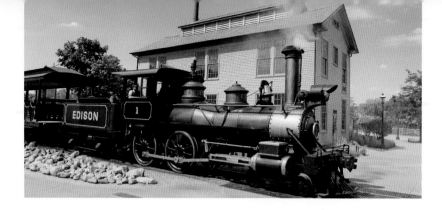

Weiser Railroad

INSPIRED BY HENRY FORD's interest in railroads, Museum staff added a three-mile, standard gauge railroad around the Village in the early 1970s. The 0-6-4T Torch Lake locomotive, acquired for the initial operation, had been used in Michigan's Upper Peninsula mining country. This standard gauge locomotive was manufactured in 1873 by the Mason Machine Works of Taunton, Massachusetts.

The Edison locomotive was based upon Civil War–era locomotives, whose small size and light weight were suited to rough track. Henry Ford commissioned this replica of a 4-4-0 standard gauge American-type locomotive in 1932, using parts that were rebuilt, restored, and replicated from an actual 1860s locomotive.

The 1897 4-4-0 standard gauge Baldwin #7 was originally used by the Detroit & Lima Northern Railway, hauling freight and passengers through Ohio and southern Michigan. Henry Ford acquired the locomotive in 1920, restored it, and made it his personal locomotive, often operating it. It was returned to operating condition in 2013 after decades of being on display in the Henry Ford Museum of American Innovation.

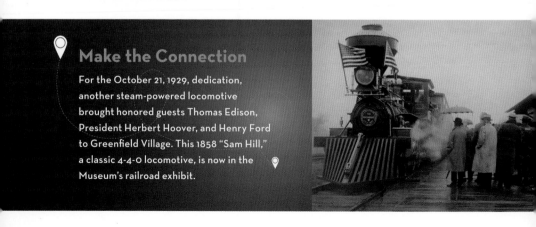

Make the Connection

For the October 21, 1929, dedication, another steam-powered locomotive brought honored guests Thomas Edison, President Herbert Hoover, and Henry Ford to Greenfield Village. This 1858 "Sam Hill," a classic 4-4-0 locomotive, is now in the Museum's railroad exhibit.

Edison Illuminating Company's Station A

AFTER TRYING HIS HAND AT VARIOUS JOBS, including a machinist, Henry Ford was hired as a steam engineer for the Edison Illuminating Company (later Detroit Edison) in Detroit. He first worked the night shift, repairing and maintaining engines at a substation, then moved to the company's main Station A plant, where he became chief engineer. It was during this time that Ford built his first car, the Quadricycle, with the help of friends and colleagues.

Through his work at Edison Illuminating Company, Henry Ford met Thomas Edison, whose brief words of support encouraged him to persevere in his automobile experiments and then try his hand at running his first automobile company. Edison would go on to become Ford's lifelong hero and friend.

Built in 1944 in Greenfield Village, Station A is something of a hybrid. It includes original equipment from the Edison Illuminating Company's A and B stations, takes architectural inspiration from the original A station, and is home to the landmark Jumbo dynamo from New York City.

LOOK CLOSER

The Jumbo dynamo, a pioneering step in direct current power generation, is the sole survivor of six engine-generating units that Edison had originally installed in his first commercial central lighting station in New York City in 1882.

A skilled glass artisan shapes a feather vase with a special tool—one of many intricate production techniques demonstrated at the Greenfield Village Glass Shop.

Liberty Craftworks

Before giant factories in cities turned out masses of identical products with precision machines and assembly-line processes, small-town mills and artisan shops hummed with activity. Farmers brought their wheat, lumber, and wool to mills; skilled workers tended to their machines in small job shops; and talented artisans produced, displayed, and sold their wares. These people contributed to the pride and industrial progress of their country villages, small towns, and emerging cities.

The Liberty Craftworks district surrounds visitors with the motion, sights, and sounds of early American manufacturing. Here, a variety of skilled artisans practice authentic techniques that are, in some cases, centuries old. These include potters, glassblowers, tinsmiths, printers, and weavers. Many of the items made here are available for purchase in Greenfield Village's on-site and online stores. In addition to artisan shops, the Liberty Craftworks district contains a number of historic mills—including a gristmill, carding mill, and sawmills—that were common in early American communities.

Gardiner Sims, an engineer and machine shop entrepreneur, helped inspire the name of the Armington & Sims Machine Shop in Greenfield Village.

Loranger Gristmill

FARMERS GREW AND HARVESTED WHEAT AND CORN, but grinding these grains by hand into flour and cornmeal was a very laborious process. Therefore, farmers were willing to carry their grain a considerable distance to have a miller do the work.

In 1832, Edward Loranger built this gristmill along the bank of Stony Creek, near Monroe, Michigan, about forty miles southwest of Detroit. Loranger Gristmill incorporated a once-groundbreaking system of grain processing and production devised by innovative millwright Oliver Evans back in the late 1700s. Evans

had replaced the traditional methods of hand carrying, pushing, and shoveling the grain with a series of more efficient elevators and conveyors. This system vastly increased production and reduced the needed workers from five to one or two.

Loranger Gristmill continued to operate until 1925, even though large commercial milling centers were replacing country mills like this one by the late 1800s. Henry Ford acquired the mill in 1928, and it opened in Greenfield Village in 1929.

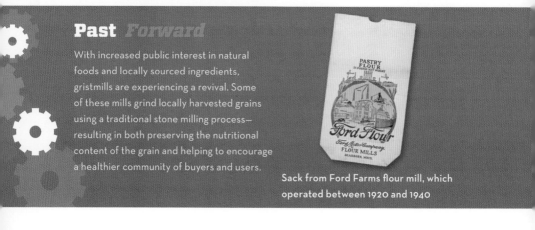

Past Forward

With increased public interest in natural foods and locally sourced ingredients, gristmills are experiencing a revival. Some of these mills grind locally harvested grains using a traditional stone milling process— resulting in both preserving the nutritional content of the grain and helping to encourage a healthier community of buyers and users.

Sack from Ford Farms flour mill, which operated between 1920 and 1940

Tripp Sawmill

SAWMILLS WERE AMONG THE FIRST MILLS established in villages and farm communities. At these sawmills, wood was cut into lumber for constructing local buildings.

The Tripp family built this steam-powered mill near the village of Tipton, Michigan (about fifty miles southwest of Detroit), in the mid-1850s. This sawmill ran for four months a year with three or four workers who cut all the lumber that local people needed for that year. The up-and-down motion of this sawmill mimics the motion of cutting lumber by hand with a large two-man pit saw.

While many sawmills were water-powered, Tripp Sawmill was steam-powered. A 20-horsepower steam engine on the ground floor provided the power for the mill.

This is one of the only surviving steam-operated up-and-down sawmills in North America. By the early 1900s, small mills like this one were forced out of business by both large-scale logging operations and long-distance rail transportation. Henry Ford purchased the mill in 1926 and used it to fabricate materials for various Greenfield Village construction projects.

Gunsolly Carding Mill

JOHN GUNSOLLY RAN THIS CARDING MILL in the 1850s and 1860s—one of several water-powered mills scattered along the banks of the winding Middle Rouge River near Plymouth, Michigan. To supplement his income, Gunsolly also ran a combination sawmill and cider mill nearby.

Carding, the process of straightening and combing wool fibers, was a fundamental step in preparing yarn to make woolen cloth. The carding machine replaced the tedious process of carding wool by hand. Carding mills operated just a few weeks each year, after farmers sheared their sheep in the spring. Henry Ford fondly remembered accompanying his father on the daylong, twenty-mile journey by horse and wagon from their home in Dearborn to this carding mill.

Did You Know?

Carding machines could produce as many rovings (loose, fluffy rolls) in one hour as a person carding by hand could accomplish in an entire day. The machine-carded rovings were also a more even thickness, making spinning more efficient.

By the 1880s, small carding mills could no longer compete with eastern and southern textile mills, where workers completed all stages of textile preparation, from carding to spinning to weaving, under one roof. In 1929, Henry Ford had this mill—by now empty and abandoned—moved to Greenfield Village.

Above: Carding machine in Gunsolly Mill

Armington & Sims Machine Shop

MACHINE SHOPS PLAYED A CRITICAL ROLE in America's industrializing society. Machinists at all-purpose job shops like this used machines to shape intricate metal parts for other machines. The metal-working machines they used here—like lathes (to produce rounded parts), milling machines (to cut gear teeth and slots), and planers (to produce flat surfaces)—shaped parts very precisely. This emphasis on precision parts is what made mass-production systems like the automobile assembly line possible.

Workers at these shops shared knowledge and ideas, helping give rise to the professions of mechanical and manufacturing engineering. At age sixteen, Henry Ford apprenticed at a machine shop in Detroit. There he acquired formative skills that would later enable him to invent his first automobile, the Quadricycle; to improve upon it with successive automobiles leading to the Model T; and to create his moving assembly line.

Built in Greenfield Village in 1929, the Armington & Sims Machine Shop and Foundry is a generalized re-creation of a small, all-purpose machine shop from the early 1900s.

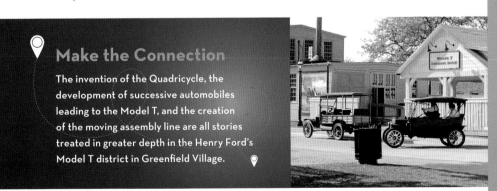

Make the Connection

The invention of the Quadricycle, the development of successive automobiles leading to the Model T, and the creation of the moving assembly line are all stories treated in greater depth in the Henry Ford's Model T district in Greenfield Village.

Printing Office

THIS SHOP IS REPRESENTATIVE OF A SMALL-TOWN PRINTING OFFICE from the 1870s or 1880s. Shops like these printed one- or two-page items like tickets, letterheads, notices, invoices, vouchers, coupons, cards, posters, and receipts. Some also produced the local weekly newspaper. Small printing shops were vital to local communities whose residents depended upon them for news as well as business, family, and personal printing needs. These offices often became informal meeting places where townspeople could discuss politics, breaking national news, and local issues.

Did You Know?

Thomas Edison and the Wright brothers all tried printing newspapers: Edison produced the single-page *Weekly Herald*, then the investigative *Paul Pry*. The Wright brothers produced the four-page *West Side News*, then *The Evening Item*, before starting their bicycle business.

While printing offices in large cities might employ over one hundred people, rural and small town offices generally had fewer than ten workers. The owner of one of these shops would most likely have been a businessman who edited the local newspaper and relied on a foreman to manage the printing operation. The foreman generally oversaw one to three on-site journeyman printers and an apprentice, along with a "tramp printer" who occasionally stopped by.

Print shop workers, about 1910

Tin Shop

THIS SHOP, BUILT IN GREENFIELD VILLAGE in 1933, represents a typical tin-smith's operation of the 1860s to 1880s era. Here, tinsmiths demonstrate their craft using a combination of hand tools and hand-operated machines.

During the 1800s, tin became the most popular material in the United States for utilitarian household items. Housewives loved these lightweight, attractive, easy-to-clean items, which quickly replaced older wood, pewter, and iron housewares.

Tinsmiths used patterns to trace shapes onto sheets of tinplate, then cut them out with heavy shears. The tin—flexible enough to be worked at room temperature—was curved and folded as needed with hammers or mallets, or shaped by hand over a small anvil called a stake. Steel punches and chisels were used to poke holes in the tin to make decorative patterns. Later, tinsmiths used more sophisticated tools and machines to increase productivity.

By the 1880s, large factories with steam-driven metal-stamping presses replaced the work of tinsmiths. These machines could do in seconds what took tin-smiths several hours to form and solder.

Tinsmiths with work tools, about 1875

Glass Shop

IN THE GLASS SHOP, skilled artisans demonstrate traditional glass production techniques. Free-blown glass production, which involves gathering and shaping molten glass on the end of a blowpipe, is most often shown. Glass artisans also demonstrate molding and shaping.

Glassworkers have historically been considered among the most talented of craftspeople because of the knowledge and skill needed to work with the material, processes, and equipment. The earliest glass used in America was imported, which was sturdier and more elegant than colonial attempts at glassmaking. In 1738, Caspar Wistar opened the first financially successful American glasshouse, in New Jersey.

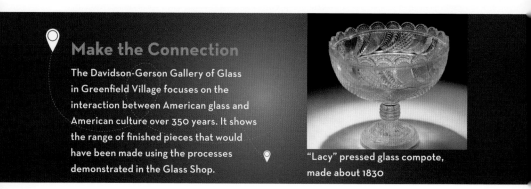

Make the Connection

The Davidson-Gerson Gallery of Glass in Greenfield Village focuses on the interaction between American glass and American culture over 350 years. It shows the range of finished pieces that would have been made using the processes demonstrated in the Glass Shop.

"Lacy" pressed glass compote, made about 1830

Most fine glass was imported from Europe through the early 1800s, while European immigrants brought their unique styles and variations of glasswork to America. At this time, American glassmakers introduced new techniques: first blowing glass into molds and then revolutionizing the industry by using mechanical glass-pressing machines to produce quantities of low-cost, affordable glass. As large factories produced inexpensive glassware in the late 1800s, some glassmakers focused on the artistic qualities of glass, which wealthy consumers used and displayed in their homes as signs of status.

Hand-blown "Lily Pad" pitcher made in the Village Glass Shop, based on early nineteenth-century American examples

The Glass Shop in Greenfield Village was built 1931–32. It was an original design named for the Boston & Sandwich Glass Company on Cape Cod, Massachusetts—a significant early producer of pressed glass. A few bricks from the original factory were brought back and incorporated into the building around the shop's doors and windows.

Pottery Shop

AT THE POTTERY SHOP, built 1939–40 in Greenfield Village, visitors can watch the complete process of pottery making, from mixing and forming clay to decorating finished products.

Red clay has been commonly used to make utilitarian items, since it hardens at a lower temperature than other clays. The development of ceramic glazes—which date back millennia—enabled pottery to hold water and other liquids for an extended period of time.

European immigrants brought the techniques and tools of their craft to America. By the mid-1800s, local, family-owned potteries had evolved into specialized shops with many workers. American potters also began to produce utilitarian products of stoneware, a dense and durable clay body that held liquids without the addition of glaze.

By the end of the 1800s, large factories had replaced small shops to mass-produce household products. The decline in utilitarian pottery making gave rise to a new art pottery movement in which different forms of pottery were appreciated more for their artistry than their function.

Weaving Shop

THE WEAVING SHOP shows the evolution of textile production from the colonial home to the commercial factory. Housed in a converted 1840s Georgia cotton gin mill, it includes one of the few operating Jacquard looms in North America.

The colonial-style loom was used to weave fabric for clothing, table and bed linens, towels, and other domestic uses. With this loom, a skilled weaver could produce one foot of fabric in an hour. The flying shuttle loom had a special attachment—invented in Great Britain in 1733—that allowed the weaver to produce up to three times more fabric per hour than the colonial-style loom.

The innovative Jacquard attachment—which came to America from Europe in the 1820s—used a continuous string of punched cards to control the lifting of individual warp threads, allowing the creation of complex patterns in the cloth.

The 1926 Crompton & Knowles power loom, used to make prototype seating upholstery for the Ford Model T, produced about twenty-five feet of worsted wool per hour.

Early nineteenth-century colonial-style loom

Past *Forward*

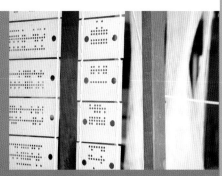

Jacquard loom punched cards are believed to have inspired the IBM punch cards that provided instructions for the first commercial computers. Evolutionary steps that led to this included English mathematician and engineer Charles Babbage's Analytical Engine of 1837, Herman Hollerith's punched-card tabulating machine for the 1890 census, and IBM's early data-processing machines.

A Jacquard loom, made in 1934 in Greenfield Village based upon historic examples

A team of Percheron draft horses assists with seasonal farm tasks at Firestone Farm.

Working Farms

The Working Farms district illustrates the story of America's agricultural heritage, from the earliest and most traditional agricultural tools on display at the Soybean Lab Agricultural Gallery to the 1880s-era Firestone Farm to Henry Ford's soybean experiments in the 1930s.

At Firestone Farm, visitors can experience the sights, sounds, and smells of a real working farm from the 1880s. Whether it's watching animals being fed, the cows being milked, the noonday dinner being prepared and served, or seasonal planting and harvesting activities, visitors can become immersed in another time—a time before almost everything people ate came from the supermarket. The crops, orchard fruits, and livestock are all true to what the Firestone family would have had on their farm.

Firestone Farm may seem like one of the most picturesque areas of Greenfield Village. But laboring on a farm each day was hard, sometimes backbreaking, work. Successive innovations that attempted to make farm work easier are displayed in the Soybean Lab Agricultural Gallery, the gateway to the Working Farms district.

The Soybean Lab in Greenfield Village about 1940, when soybeans were grown there for processing

Soybean Lab
Agricultural Gallery

THIS BUILDING, ONCE CALLED THE SOYBEAN EXPERIMENTAL LABORATORY, was the first place in which soybeans were processed into plastic for industrial uses.

Henry Ford was convinced that agricultural crops could be used for industrial purposes, especially for making car parts. In this building, scientists experimented with crops such as cantaloupes, tomatoes, turnips, and rutabagas before deciding that soybeans showed the most promise for industrial use. Soybean oil made superior paint enamel and lubricants. Soy-based plastics could be molded into horn buttons, gearshift knobs, door handles, window trim, and accelerator pedals. Ford envisioned entire cars in which every part was made of a soybean derivative!

Constructed 1929–30 in Greenfield Village, this building still contains original soybean processing equipment as well as a model soybean oil extractor that

once demonstrated how the real six-ton extractor unit in the lab worked.

Today, the Soybean Lab Agricultural Gallery houses agricultural tools and equipment from The Henry Ford's collection. These tools, ranging from traditional forms to innovative designs, made farm work faster and easier.

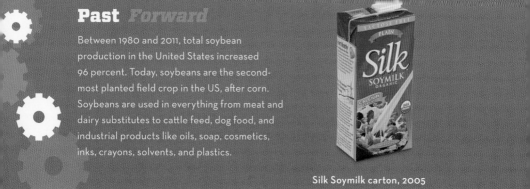

Past *Forward*

Between 1980 and 2011, total soybean production in the United States increased 96 percent. Today, soybeans are the second-most planted field crop in the US, after corn. Soybeans are used in everything from meat and dairy substitutes to cattle feed, dog food, and industrial products like oils, soap, cosmetics, inks, crayons, solvents, and plastics.

Silk Soymilk carton, 2005

The Horses of Greenfield Village

BEFORE AUTOMOBILES AND OTHER MOTORIZED VEHICLES became the norm, horses were ubiquitous in towns, villages, and farms. In Greenfield Village, horses provide a means of transport as well as a source of labor on the working Firestone Farm.

One of the best places to see the horses is near the Village entrance, by Richart Wagon Shop, where visitors wait to be shuttled on an omnibus or carriage. But horses appear throughout the Village year-round—at private weddings, as the mount for the 1905 US Forest Ranger in the summer, as the means for carrying Ichabod Crane away from the Headless Horseman during the Hallowe'en program in October, and for pulling the wagons that carry visitors through the Village during Holiday Nights.

Horses also provide the power needed for activities at Firestone Farm. In the 1880s, the Firestones would have had a team of draft horses—most likely Percherons—for plowing and heavy chores. The Firestones also had a team of light carriage or riding horses, probably Morgans.

Did You Know?

The Percheron was the most common draft horse in the United States in the 1800s. These intelligent and hardworking horses, originally bred as warhorses, have appeared multiple times in the Tournament of Roses parade in Pasadena, California.

Firestone Farm

FIRESTONE FARM IS A LIVING HISTORY RE-CREATION of what life was like on Benjamin and Catherine Firestone's 118-acre farm near the village of Columbiana in east central Ohio in the 1880s. The ever-present work around the farm changes seasonally. Pasture, oats, hay, field corn, winter wheat, and an apple orchard occupy much of the farm's seven acres in Greenfield Village.

Like other farmers in the area, Benjamin Firestone mixed traditional and more up-to-date farming practices. For example, corn was planted with a traditional hand planter while wheat was planted with a horse-drawn grain drill that became popular in the 1850s.

Benjamin Firestone continued to raise wrinkly Merino sheep as his father, Peter, had done. Back in Peter's time, area farmers had realized huge profits from raising pure-bred Merino sheep, which produced the finest grade of wool in the world. By the time Benjamin ran the farm in the 1880s, however, competition from wool growers elsewhere was dramatically cutting into his and other farmers'

Benjamin Firestone, about 1875

LOOK CLOSER

The sheep at Firestone Farm have a wrinkly, heavy fleece. During the 1880s, farmers bred Merino sheep with particularly wrinkly or heavily folded skin because the heavier fleece of these Merinos yielded higher profits.

profits. But he and his neighbors continued to raise Merinos as they had always done. These farmers would soon face a financial crisis, forcing them to gradually shift their livestock away from sheep toward a greater emphasis on beef or dairy cattle. Watching this and other economic crises on his father Benjamin's farm convinced young Harvey—the future tire industrialist—to leave the farm behind and seek his fortune in the city.

Past *Forward*

The fruits and vegetables grown at Firestone Farm are heirloom varieties. Steeped in flavor, texture, and traditions, they replicate authentic varieties of the 1880s. In fact, the foods grown and produced here fit right in with today's local food and farm-to-table movements, which advocate localized farming and food distribution practices.

Firestone Farmhouse

BENJAMIN AND CATHERINE FIRESTONE raised their three sons in this farm-house, including second son Harvey, who later founded Firestone Tire & Rubber Company. They were the third generation of Firestones to live here.

The brick farmhouse was built in 1828 on the Firestone farmstead in east central Ohio. In 1882, the Firestone family made major updates to their house. At that time, the traditional Pennsylvania German layout was transformed with a small foyer inside the front entrance; separate dining room, sitting room, kitchen, and pantry

Did You Know?

In 1882, fourteen-year-old Harvey and his friend James Maxwell secretly stuck a signed and dated note in the ceiling above the central stairway. Finding this note helped Museum staff pinpoint the date of the house remodeling.

This handwritten note was found during the dismantling of the farmhouse at its original site in 1983–84.

spaces; fashionable wallpaper; and new, up-to-date furniture. The extensive remodel embodied the family's steady transition from following older Pennsylvania German customs to embracing a new mainstream American culture.

Firestone Farm on its original site in Columbiana, Ohio, about 1876

The cooking and domestic chores in this farmhouse replicate those of the Firestone family in the 1880s. A daily midday dinner for the farm staff is prepared using authentic recipes. Food-related activities shift with the seasons, from planting the kitchen garden in the spring to canning fruits in the summer to making sauerkraut in the fall. The cellar storage room is stocked with preserves, barrels of sauerkraut, and bacon and sausage from hogs butchered on the farm.

Although they Americanized their home, the Firestones' food traditions persisted. Daily meals prepared at the house today reflect the family's ancestral Pennsylvania German diet—the interplay between sweet, tart, and salty flavors.

T3E34

F-150 truck bodies on the assembly line

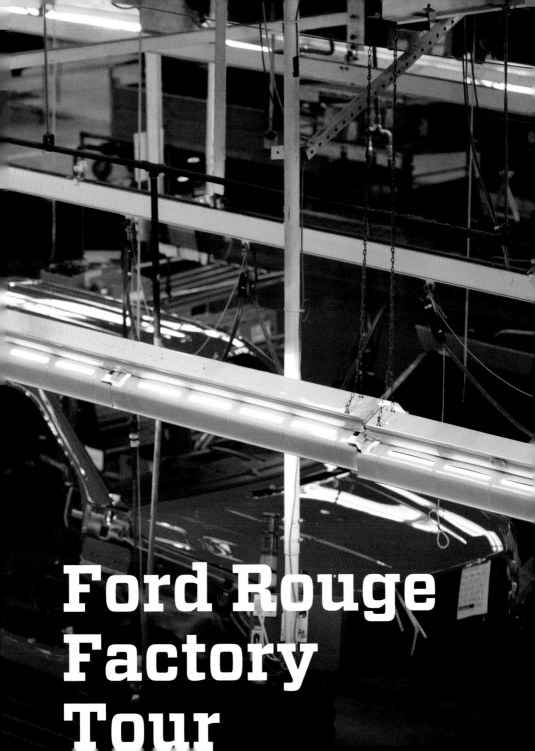

Ford Rouge Factory Tour

"Ford Rouge Center ... honors the legacy of innovation established by my great-grandfather."
—Bill Ford Jr., executive chairman of Ford Motor Company and Henry Ford's great-grandson

Ford Rouge Factory Tour

The historic Ford Rouge Center dates back to 1915, when Henry Ford began to create the world's largest single industrial complex. When assembly-line production started at the Rouge in 1927, visitors marveled as tons of iron ore, coal, and sand poured into one end and finished cars rolled out the other—the very next day. By the time public tours ended there in 1980, times had changed. Ford's vision of a unified manufacturing complex had become outmoded.

In 1999, Bill Ford Jr. made a dramatic announcement. The new Ford Rouge Center—now a six-hundred-acre site—would undergo a $2 billion transformation. Its centerpiece would be an entirely new truck assembly plant designed for flexibility, efficiency, and sustainability. These characteristics have come to define twenty-first-century manufacturing.

A new era of Rouge tours—in partnership with The Henry Ford—began in 2004 with the production of Ford F-150 trucks. The self-guided experience includes the Legacy Theater, recounting the Ford Rouge Center's history; the Manufacturing Innovation Theater, a multisensory exploration of the manufacturing experience; the Assembly Plant Walking Tour, featuring a view of the final assembly process of the latest Ford F-150s; an Observation Deck to view the Ford Rouge Center's innovative environmental features; and the Legacy Gallery, displaying five historic vehicles manufactured at the Rouge.

The Legacy Gallery at Ford Rouge Factory Tour features such iconic vehicles as the 1956 Thunderbird, opposite.

Legacy Theater

THE LEGACY THEATER connects Henry Ford's original vision for innovative manufacturing with the company's ongoing legacy of revitalization and reinvention.

Ford Motor Company already dominated the American automotive industry after introducing the Model T (1908), the working assembly line at Ford's Highland Park Plant (1913), and the unprecedented doubling of workers' pay to five dollars a day (1914). But Henry Ford was planning something even bigger: a vast manufacturing complex for producing automobiles from raw material to finished product. Later called "vertical integration," this idea would set the standard for American manufacturing.

Did You Know?

World War I impeded Henry Ford's efforts to get the River Rouge complex up and running. Instead, he attempted—with mixed results—to apply his mass-production techniques to the construction of submarine-chasing naval vessels called Eagle Boats.

An aerial view of the Ford Rouge Plant with boat docks and bins with raw materials, 1948

Ford Service Department men confront UAW organizers at Miller Road Overpass, May 26, 1937. The incident became known as the Battle of the Overpass.

In 1915, Ford began buying land in an undeveloped area along the winding Rouge River, southwest of Detroit, which provided access to transportation networks and room for expansion. During the 1920s, the River Rouge complex took shape much as Henry Ford had envisioned. Outside observers marveled at its vast scope and scale.

As Henry Ford became obsessed with keeping car prices down during the Great Depression of the 1930s, work on the assembly line accelerated at an unremitting pace. Increasingly, workers felt that speaking with a single voice—as part of the growing union

This famous image of the Ford Rouge Plant in 1927, taken by Charles Sheeler, is considered an icon of modern photography.

movement—was their only hope for change. Henry Ford tried to fight that change for years until he finally relented and the Rouge workers voted to join the United Automobile Workers (UAW) union in 1941. The new partnership between labor and management would prove to be one of the company's greatest assets.

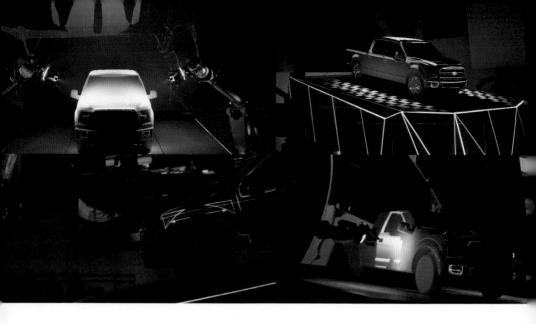

Manufacturing Innovation: Theater and Plant Tour

THE HIGH-ENERGY MANUFACTURING INNOVATION THEATER offers a fitting introduction to the integrated processes that visitors can see inside the Ford F-150 truck assembly plant. This special-effects theater experience takes viewers from initial customer research through the drive-out of a new aluminum-body F-150 truck.

On a one-third-mile elevated walkway, visitors can view the final assembly and testing of F-150s at the Dearborn Truck Plant (DTP): the "build" (assembling of components) of the door and truck box; the "install" (installation) of such parts as the instrument panel and windshield; and the "decking" (reconnection) of the truck cab and box. Flow diagrams are posted to help visitors understand the movement of vehicle parts through the plant. The complex web of equipment, robotics, parts delivery, and skilled workers makes it possible for one truck per minute to be assembled at full line speeds.

The DTP incorporates state-of-the-art manufacturing processes. Assembly lines are flexible enough to handle three different vehicle

Did You Know?

If an employee sees an issue with the build, he or she can stop the line and speak up. Other quality tracking devices are built into the tools and visible in the Customer Acceptance final testing area.

platforms and nine different models at the same time, allowing a quick change of the models that are produced at a given time as customer demand dictates.

The assembly plant's design considers the needs of people as well as machinery—a legacy handed down from Henry Ford and his preferred architect Albert Kahn, who designed many of the original Rouge buildings. Employee comfort and safety features include skylights, windows, an air tempering system, and adjustable skillet (pallet) conveyors for each vehicle with individualized ergonomic height settings.

Legacy Gallery

THE LEGACY GALLERY features a display of five legendary historic vehicles that were made at the Rouge, along with the latest aluminum-body F-150 truck.

Although Model T components were manufactured at the Rouge, the Model A was the first automobile to be assembled here. Beginning in 1927, nearly five million of these automobiles were sold over the next four model years.

In 1932, Henry Ford insisted on incorporating an affordable V-8 engine into new vehicle models to upstage Chevrolet's low-priced inline-6. By casting this engine's crankcase and cylinders as a single unit, Ford cut production costs and held his vehicle's starting price to under $500. Ford's original V-8 engine design stayed in production until 1953.

Ford's 1949 model was the company's first all-new car after World War II. Its "envelope" body, with integral fenders and smooth slab sides, was a departure from previous designs.

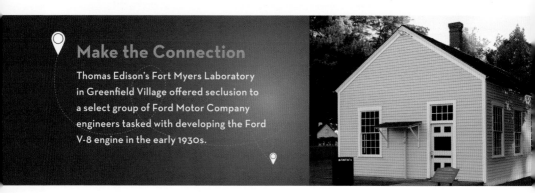

Make the Connection

Thomas Edison's Fort Myers Laboratory in Greenfield Village offered seclusion to a select group of Ford Motor Company engineers tasked with developing the Ford V-8 engine in the early 1930s.

1965 Ford Mustang convertible

The Thunderbird, introduced in October 1954, combined a sporty feel with the comfortable appointments of a prestige model. Within ten days, orders for the T-Bird soared above all expectations.

The 1965 Ford Mustang is one of the most significant vehicles built at the Rouge. With its sporty look, reasonable price, and numerous options, this car appealed to a wide cross section of buyers. More than one million Mustangs were sold within two years of the car's April 1964 introduction. Mustangs were produced at the Rouge until 2004.

LOOK CLOSER

The "spinner" in the center of the 1949 Coupe's grille suggested an airplane propeller—an early example of the aviation themes that characterized postwar American cars. Similarly, the Thunderbird's aerodynamic design was inspired by jet aircraft.

Observation Deck

THE EIGHTY-FOOT-HIGH OBSERVATION DECK offers the perfect opportunity for visitors to draw connections between old and new at the Ford Rouge Center. The view south (on the left) looks on buildings that survive from Henry Ford's original Rouge complex as well as newer structures that are integral to today's F-150 truck production.

The Observation Deck provides unique views of the Ford Rouge Center's environmental innovations. When Henry Ford transformed the natural wetlands along the Rouge River into his great industrial complex, he unwittingly created over time a polluted brownfield site. During the 1990s, the aging Rouge could have been abandoned. But Bill Ford decided to reenvision it, influenced by the pioneering environmental work of architect Bill McDonough. Together, they saw a site that could become healthy again, a place where songbirds would be one of the metrics of success.

At six hundred acres, the Ford Rouge Center site is the largest brownfield redevelopment in the United States. Special features include a Gold-certified LEED (Leadership in Energy and Environmental Design) Visitor Center; an all-natural

Top: Photovoltaic (solar) panels on the Visitor Center roof; above: heat-exchanging solar array cuts energy use in the Visitor Center.

storm water treatment system with one of the world's largest living roofs (planted with sedum, a perennial ground cover); a paint plant that captures fumes to create fuel cells; and natural plantings to treat decades of soil pollution.

A Living Laboratory walking tour, offered seasonally, gives visitors a chance to see sustainable design and new land use in action.

Past *Forward*

The living roof at the Dearborn Truck Plant, a pioneering idea in 2004, has since been incorporated into thousands of building complexes worldwide. Today, "green roofs" adorn everything from doghouses and homes to manufacturing, commercial, government, and university buildings.

Living roof at Ford Rouge Center

A scene from the Museum's
Driving America exhibition

Giant Screen Experience

HERE, GUESTS CAN EXPERIENCE SOME OF THE MOST ENTERTAINING and enlightening stories of America's past, present, and future ever told—in one of the nation's most impressive venues for telling them. The Henry Ford Giant Screen Experience delivers a year-round calendar of programming geared to exploring the people, places, themes, and ideas that bring the American Experience to life—all in a cinema environment enhanced by state-of-the-art projection, sound, and seating.

Did You Know?

The Giant Screen Experience at The Henry Ford is eighty feet by forty-four feet in size and has 4K digital projection—the ultimate evolution of moving-picture technology in which Thomas Edison played a foundational role.

Since the Giant Screen Experience is located outside the entrance to the Henry Ford Museum of American Innovation, moviegoers do not need a ticket to the Museum to see a film. Showtimes run throughout the day. Discounts are available for advance reservations for groups of fifteen or more. For more information, hours, and pricing, visit www.thehenryford.org/giantscreen.

Benson Ford Research Center

AN OPEN TREASURY OF RESEARCH, HISTORICAL EXPERTISE, and unparalleled collections, Benson Ford Research Center is the place to personally access the archives, records, and collections that document the American Experience. The Research Center holds business records, product and trade literature, manuscripts, books, prints, maps, photographs, and several special collections. It maintains the largest and most significant collections in the United States concerning the impact of the automobile, industrial manufacturing and design, and other aspects of American culture and everyday life.

The Reading Room is open on weekdays to assist guests with history research, provide access to historic documents and rare books, and conduct behind-the-scenes tours. The General Tour explores precious collections, including Thomas Edison's patent models and research papers, Henry Ford's office papers, folk art, domestic artifacts and textiles, and couture fashion. Other tours include the Conservation Laboratory Tour and the Early Days of Photography Tour. All tours are available for a fee and are scheduled through The Henry Ford's Call Center.

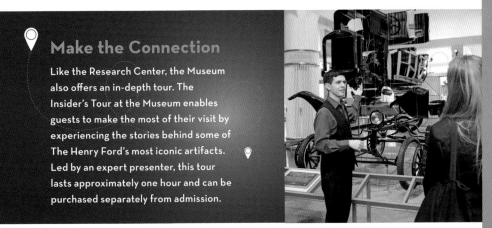

Make the Connection

Like the Research Center, the Museum also offers an in-depth tour. The Insider's Tour at the Museum enables guests to make the most of their visit by experiencing the stories behind some of The Henry Ford's most iconic artifacts. Led by an expert presenter, this tour lasts approximately one hour and can be purchased separately from admission.

Suggested Itineraries

TWO-DAY TRIP

The Henry Ford offers four unique attractions: Henry Ford Museum of American Innovation, Greenfield Village, the Ford Rouge Factory Tour, and the Giant Screen Experience. In order to see as much as possible, try to set aside two days for your trip. On day one, visit the Henry Ford Museum of American Innovation and the Ford Rouge Factory Tour. Then tour Greenfield Village the following day. During your visit to the Village, you may want to take a break inside, in the comfort of the Giant Screen Experience, and watch a thirty- or forty-five-minute film.

Day One

HENRY FORD MUSEUM OF AMERICAN INNOVATION

The Museum opens at 9:30 a.m. If you'd like to start with a guided overview, you can choose a one-hour Insider's Tour from an expert presenter. If you'd rather take things at your own speed, you can see some of the highlights listed below. Grab lunch from one of the eateries. Be sure to have your tickets in hand for the last Ford Rouge Factory Tour bus, which leaves promptly at 3:00 p.m. and returns by 5:00 p.m.

Museum Highlights

* denotes recommended must-sees.

Agriculture
- #1 Fordson Tractor
- Sperry-New Holland Combine (climb-in activity)

With Liberty and Justice for All
- Rosa Parks Bus*
- Copy of Declaration of Independence
- Lincoln Chair*

Heroes of the Sky
- 1939 Douglas DC-3
- Ford Tri-Motor Airplane
- Sikorsky Helicopter

Made in America: Manufacturing

- Build a Model T (hands-on activity)

Made in America: Power

- Corliss Stationary Steam Engine

Fully Furnished

- Eames Prototype Chair
- Marshmallow Sofa

Driving America

- 1931 Bugatti Royale
- Drive-In Theater (10-minute films)
- Goldenrod
- Mustang 1
- Quadricycle*

Presidential Vehicles

- Kennedy Limousine*
- FDR "Sunshine Special"

Railroads

- Allegheny Locomotive* (climb-in activity)
- Fairlane Railcar

Other Exhibits

- Dymaxion House*
- Mathematica*
- Davidson-Gerson Modern Glass Gallery*
- Apple 1 Computer*

Dining

- Lamy's Diner
- Michigan Café

FORD ROUGE FACTORY TOUR

In the midafternoon, catch the bus from the circle drive in front of the Museum to visit the Ford Rouge Factory Tour, where you can see modern manufacturing innovation in action, including real-time Ford F-150 production. The Rouge is a fifteen-minute ride from The Henry Ford. Buses to the Rouge depart every twenty minutes. Tickets can be purchased at the Welcome Center. The last bus leaves the Henry Ford Museum of American Innovation promptly at 3:00 p.m. and returns by 5:00 p.m.

Tour Highlights

- Legacy Theater
- Manufacturing Innovation Theater
- Observation Deck
- Assembly Plant

Day Two

GREENFIELD VILLAGE (open seasonally)

Spend your second day at The Henry Ford touring three hundred years of American life in Greenfield Village. Start when the gates open, at 9:30 a.m. There are eighty acres and eighty-three authentic structures in the Village, with transportation and rides. Take a train ride in the morning while touring the historic sites. Then grab lunch in one of the dining establishments and ride in a Model T or horse-drawn omnibus in the afternoon. Rides can be purchased separately from general admission. Guests can also ride all day with an unlimited pass.

Village Highlights

* denotes recommended must-sees.

Working Farms
- Firestone Farm and Farmhouse*

Liberty Craftworks
- Glass Shop*
- Pottery Shop*

Railroad Junction
- DT&M Roundhouse
- Smiths Creek Depot

Main Street
- Logan County Courthouse
- Cohen Millinery
- Wright Cycle Shop*

Henry Ford's Model T
- Ford Home*

Edison at Work
- Thomas Edison's Menlo Park Complex*
- Sarah Jordan Boarding House

Porches and Parlors
- Susquehanna Plantation
- Daggett Farmhouse*
- Noah Webster Home
- Mattox Family Home*

Transportation and Rides
- Model AA Bus
- Model T*
- Carriage
- Railroad
- Carousel

Dining
- A Taste of History
- Eagle Tavern

ONE-DAY TRIP

If you're only able to spend one day at The Henry Ford, split your time between Henry Ford Museum of American Innovation and Greenfield Village, touring the Museum for half the day and the Village for the other half, using your best judgment based on the weather. Both the Museum and the Village open at 9:30 a.m. and close at 5:00 p.m.

Tips and Information

Calendar: While the Museum, Giant Screen Experience, and Ford Rouge Factory Tour are open all year, the Village is open daily from April 15 through October 31, on weekends in November, and on select evenings in December. It is closed from January 1 through April 14. The Weiser Railroad operates daily from April 15 through October 31.

Getting Around: The Henry Ford is expansive. Bring comfortable shoes. Take care when crossing the streets of the Village, where historic vehicles, antique bicycles, horse-drawn vehicles, and trains operate.

Food and Drink: The Henry Ford has many on-site dining and concession options, from quick bites to full-course culinary feasts. Beer and wine are available for purchase at select locations.

Animals: Pets are not permitted, but certified service animals are allowed. Please note that service animals will be in close proximity to animals in Greenfield Village, including horses, sheep, and chickens.

Personal Mobility-Assistance Items: Children's strollers or small wagons are permitted, as are motorized wheelchairs, electric scooters, and wheelchairs. Strollers, wagons, wheelchairs, and scooters are available for rent in various facilities. Bicycles, tricycles, recreational scooters, in-line skates, and roller skates are not allowed.

Wheelchair Accessibility: Public entrances are wheelchair accessible. All Museum exhibits are wheelchair accessible except for the interiors of the Allegheny cab, combine cab, Rosa Parks bus, and Dymaxion House. Wheelchairs are admitted into the historic buildings at Greenfield Village whenever possible.

Sensory Sensitivities: Noise-canceling headphones, earplugs, and a communication board are available at the Welcome Center ticket desk and the Greenfield Village ticket building. Earplugs are available at the Manufacturing Innovation Theater at the Ford Rouge Factory Tour.

Have a Question? Call ahead of your visit, especially if you need to request a special accommodation, at 313.982.6001. Our Call Center is open seven days a week.

Group Visits

EDUCATORS AND GROUP LEADERS can access free pre- and post-visit classroom resources as well as scavenger hunts, itineraries, and other field trip aids. Innovative educators can inspire tomorrow's change makers with new curricula focusing on creative problem solving through lessons in innovation and entrepreneurship. Special seasonal field trip programs are also available for a more focused learning adventure.

An award-winning venue, The Henry Ford is the region's number one place to host private events, including weddings, conventions, corporate celebrations, and group picnics. Certified event planners offer a full range of services and venues for groups of up to five thousand guests.

Did You Know?

The largest category of group visits to The Henry Ford is school field trips. The Henry Ford hosts approximately two hundred thousand school-aged children each year, ranging from pre-kindergarten to high school students.

Special Events

THE HENRY FORD OFFERS A VARIETY OF SPECIAL EVENTS throughout the year. Most are free with admission to the Museum or Village, and all are family friendly. Visit www.thehenryford.org for current and future events, or contact the Call Center at 313.982.6001 for more information.

Listed are some of The Henry Ford's most popular events:

MOTOR MUSTER (JUNE)

Motor Muster celebrates automobiles, from the glamorous classics of the 1930s to the brawny muscle cars of the 1970s. During this weekend event, Greenfield Village is filled with classic cars, vintage trucks, motorcycles, military vehicles, bicycles, and fire engines. There's also a live musical show on Saturday night.

MAKER FAIRE DETROIT (JULY)

Maker Faire Detroit at The Henry Ford includes everything from robotics, electronics, and science to food, music, and fashion. Here, hundreds of makers demonstrate their inventions and creativity each year.

HISTORIC BASE BALL (AUGUST)

At the annual World Tournament of Historic Base Ball, players aren't allowed to wear gloves or pitch overhand, and spitting is highly discouraged. Clubs must play by the same rules as when the Detroit Base Ball Club hosted the World's Base Ball Tournament in 1867. The champion club receives $300, and a bag of peanuts goes to the club with the least number of victories.

OLD CAR FESTIVAL (SEPTEMBER)

Greenfield Village's Old Car Festival features hundreds of vehicles from the 1890s through 1932. At America's longest-running antique car show, guests can talk to car owners, watch driving games, see a Model T assembled in minutes, and listen to car talks with experts. Saturday night also features a live musical show.

HALLOWE'EN (OCTOBER)

During Hallowe'en, guests can stroll down Village streets and alleys haunted by over one thousand carved jack-o'-lanterns—stretching over a mile long—and lavishly costumed characters. There are dancing skeletons, witches and wizards, and vaudeville acts that include sword-swallowing and fire-breathing. This gathering is kid friendly and nightmare-free.

HOLIDAY NIGHTS (DECEMBER)

Holiday Nights in Greenfield Village takes guests on a lantern-lit journey into a living snow globe filled with live music, skating, and fireworks. There are candlelit windows, roasting chestnuts, carolers, sleigh bells, along with Santa and his live reindeer. Guests can ride in a horse-drawn wagon or a Model T.

Did You Know?

Holiday Nights is the most popular holiday event in the region. *USA TODAY* calls it one of the "top 10 places to take the grandchildren."

Index

The Henry Ford® in Dearborn, Michigan, is an internationally recognized cultural destination that brings the past forward by immersing visitors in the stories of ingenuity, resourcefulness, and innovation that helped shape America.

A National Historic Landmark with an unparalleled collection of artifacts from three hundred years of American history, The Henry Ford is a force for sparking curiosity and inspiring tomorrow's innovators. More than 1.6 million visitors annually experience its four venues: Henry Ford Museum of American Innovation™, Greenfield Village®, Ford Rouge Factory Tour, and the Benson Ford Research Center®. A continually expanding array of content available at www.thehenryford.org provides anytime, anywhere access to The Henry Ford Archive of American Innovation®. The Henry Ford is also home to Henry Ford Academy, a public charter high school that educates 485 students a year on the institution's campus.

In 2014, The Henry Ford premiered its first-ever national television series, *The Henry Ford's Innovation Nation*, a two-time Emmy® Award winner showcasing present-day change makers and The Henry Ford's artifacts and unique guest experiences. Hosted by news correspondent and humorist Mo Rocca, it airs Saturday mornings on CBS.

Author: Donna R. Braden, Curator of Public Life
Publishing Manager: Terri L. Anderson, Senior
    Director of Business Development and Licensing

ACKNOWLEDGMENTS
The author wishes to acknowledge the Curatorial, Historical Resources, Program, and Creative Services staff at The Henry Ford—past and present—whose writings, expertise, review, and comments helped in the creation of this guidebook.

All images in this guidebook were supplied courtesy of The Henry Ford except the following: Page 149: iStock.com/stockstudioX

www.thf.org

The Henry Ford: Official Guidebook was developed by Beckon Books in cooperation with The Henry Ford. Beckon develops and publishes custom books for leading cultural attractions, corporations, and nonprofit organizations. Beckon Books is an imprint of Southwestern Publishing Group, Inc., 2451 Atrium Way, Nashville, Tennessee 37214. Southwestern Publishing Group, Inc., is a wholly owned subsidiary of Southwestern, Inc., Nashville, Tennessee.

Christopher G. Capen, President, Southwestern
    Publishing Group
Kristin Stephany, Director of Partner Development,
    Southwestern Publishing Group
Betsy Holt, Publisher, Beckon Books
Vicky Shea, Senior Art Director
Kristin Connelly, Managing Editor
Jennifer Benson, Proofreader
www.swpublishinggroup.com | 800-358-0560

ISBN: 978-1-935442-61-5

Printed in China

10 9 8 7 6 5 4 3 2